# The Tragedy of the Sack of Cabrières

Medieval & Renaissance
Texts and Studies

Volume 584

French Renaissance Texts in Translation

Volume 4

# The Tragedy of the Sack of Cabrières

*Translated with an introduction by*

Charles-Louis Morand-Métivier

**ACMRS PRESS**

Tempe, Arizona
2022

Arizona Center
for Medieval &
Renaissance Studies

Published by ACMRS (Arizona Center for Medieval and Renaissance Studies)
Tempe, Arizona
©2022 Arizona Board of Regents for Arizona State University.
All Rights Reserved.
ISBN: 978-0-86698-644-1

∞
*Printed in the United States of America*

*Pour Karen, Malo, et Clément, pour toujours*

# CONTENTS

| | |
|---|---|
| *Acknowledgments* | *ix* |
| *Introduction* | *xi* |
| The Waldensian Creed: From the Middle Ages to the Reformation | 1 |
| The Waldensians in Provence: Origins and History | 11 |
| Analyzing *Cabrières*: Religion, Community, Violence | 21 |
| Editing the Manuscript | 39 |
| Tragedy of the Sack of Cabrières | 45 |
| *Bibliography* | 253 |

# ACKNOWLEDGMENTS

This edition and translation of the *Tragedy of the Sack of Cabrières* is the product of many years of research and work on this play. In 2009, as I was preparing my dissertation prospectus at the University of Pittsburgh, Todd Reeser, one of my co-advisors (with Renate Blumenfeld-Kosinski) suggested that I take a look at this play. Little did I know then that many years later, I would have written its first critical edition and translation in English, which will hopefully be helpful to both specialists and non-specialists.

I would never have been able to complete this work without the help of many people. Todd and Renate were the first ones to witness my "experimentations" on this play; I want to warmly thank them for their expertise, patience, and professionalism. Janet Whatley, my predecessor at the University of Vermont, was a tremendous help while I was preparing my translation. Kathleen Long read the whole manuscript when I was revising it, and gave me previous advice, as well as time, friendship, and professionalism. Louisa Mackenzie read parts of what would become "Analyzing *Cabrières*: Religion, Community, Violence;" her feedback was extremely helpful to better frame my ideas. Bruce Hayes, Jeff Kendrick, Kitty Maynard, Scott Francis, this would never have been possible without your great support and the fantastic "apéros" we've had throughout the years, in Paris or during our stays at conferences. I also want to warmly thank Philip Usher, who first convinced me to submit an abstract for the project, and who was always a fantastic supporter of the work we authors have produced, even during very dark moments. I want to thank the wonderful staff at ACMRS, and particularly Roy Rukkila, for their constant support and quick responses to my questions. The two peer reviewers of my project gave me great feedback, which tremendously helped me with my revisions. I also want to thank my colleagues at the University of Vermont, who have witnessed the evolution of my work on a daily basis since my hire in 2013.

This project was made possible through the work of great, dedicated library staff that helped me collect the important sources needed for such a task. I specifically want to thank the librarians at the Howe Library at the University of Vermont for the quickness with which they ordered books for me, for their willingness to allow me to borrow volumes that sometimes were in-library only, as well as for their kindness and availability. I extend my gratitude to Mrs. Martina Gromesova and Sophie Vié who helped me navigate through the rich catalog of the library of the Société pour l'Histoire du Protestantisme Français. I also would like to thank the Special Collections librarians of Hillman Library at the University of Pittsburgh, at the Archives Départementales d'Indre et Loire, at the Bibliothèque Municipale de Tours, and at the Bibliothèque Nationale de France. I also want to thank Daniela Boccassini and Gabriel Audisio, who have always given of their precious time to answer my questions on their scholarship.

But the three people without whom I would never have finished this work are those who are the worthiest of praise. My wife, Karen Adams, a fantastic scholar, who made me a better scholar, and an even better man. Thank you for coping with my doubts, anxieties, and fears; thank you for your constant support, and for knowing when I needed to watch a video of cute baby animals to feel better. Thank you, Malo and Clément; you are my most significant achievements. No book I ever write will ever be as perfect as you are.

# Introduction

In April 1542, a series of attacks in the French region of the Luberon in south-western France, led by royal troops and troops from their allies of Provence, destroyed Waldensian villages. Their populations were either killed or displaced, their belongings looted, and the signs of their presence essentially erased. Even though these events were widely reported at the time, the *Tragedy of the Sack of Cabrières* is the only play devoted to the events.

In this edition, I want to do more than just translate the text into English. I want to "translate" the representation of the event and its importance in the narrative of religious persecutions in sixteenth-century France. In that sense, I will focus on a historical analysis of the play, by explaining how history is dramatized in the play. I intend this work to be not only a translation and a work of literary scholarship; I envision it as an analysis of the literary, political, and religious production of this period, a multidisciplinary analysis of Waldensianism in southeastern France. I am interested in demonstrating how this community, widely accepted by the Catholic population, having been living peacefully in the Luberon for centuries, and actively participating in the economic life of the region, suddenly became the enemy who had to be eliminated.

I have divided my edition into sections that will allow the reader to understand why Cabrières matters in the context of pre–civil war France. The first part, entitled "The Waldensian Creed: From the Middle Ages to the Reformation," focuses on the origins of the movement, from 1132 to the installation of the communities in Provence, and their subsequent incorporation in more traditional Calvinist movements. Chapter 2, "The Waldensians in Provence: Origins and History," explains the march to the destruction of the villages. I study the evolution of the royal threat and how the different edicts and orders were first ignored before they were enforced. I also study how the tension grew in the Luberon, and how it eventually blew up into the events leading to the eradication of the two villages. Chapter 3, "Analyzing *Cabrières*: Religion, Community, Violence," is a textual and analytical study of the various themes and ideas present in the text. I specifically focus on the emotionology of the text and how the communities at play in the text (the Waldensians and the Catholics) are constructed on the basis of the emotions they share. Because the theme of the play is eminently religious, I also analyze the different approaches of the Catholics (for whom religion is perceived mostly as a context for their thirst for the massacre) and the Waldensians

xii *Introduction*

(for which religion is the cornerstone of their identity). Chapter 4, "Editing the Manuscript," examines the different versions of the text—both manuscript and contemporary—and gives insight into the methodology used in establishing the edition and translation.

Following these introductory chapters, the core of the text and its translation come next. Both the transcription of the text (left) and its translation (right) are facing each other so that the reader can have direct access to the manuscript. The many translation notes help the reader navigate through the different layers of the text, from religious references, textual analysis, mention of historical events, etc. I finish this edition with a bibliography, which I hope to be as complete as possible, addressing the different issues discussed by the translation. I collected, of course, a list of all the scholarship on *Cabrières*; I also provide a list of essential works devoted to the history, theology, and politics of Waldensianism, as well as a list of books relating the massacre itself.

Unless otherwise noted, every translation of primary and secondary sources is mine. All biblical quotations come from the New King James Version. Parts of chapter 3 were previously published as "La Construction de la masculinité dans la *Tragédie du sac de Cabrières*: Le cas d'Opède," *Modern Languages Open* 1, no. 10 (2018): 1–14, doi:10.3828/mlo.v0i0.171. I want to thank the editors of *Modern Languages Open* who authorized me to use it here.

# THE WALDENSIAN CREED:
# FROM THE MIDDLE AGES TO THE REFORMATION

The Middle Ages and the Renaissance were fertile ground for heretical movements defying the orthodoxy of the church.[1] If Catharism or, later on, the Protestant Reformation are widely known to the general population, many others are still scarcely studied.[2] Waldensianism is one of these lesser-known heresies. Yet, it is one of the oldest still in existence, with its roots tracing back to the twelfth century. Because of a few core ideas in common with later movements, it is often perceived as being "the Reformation before the Reformation." However, simply seeing Waldensianism through this lens would be reductive. In this chapter, I will focus on the creation of the movement and on its evolution leading it to become part of the Reformation.[3]

Waldensianism as a religious movement originated from a small group of people, the Poor of Lyons. They were organized around the tutelary figure of Pierre Vaudès, whose persona is still shrouded in mystery.[4] Many discussions have arisen about his name, as it appears under many different forms.[5] It is not

---

[1] See Walter Bauer, *Orthodoxy and Heresy in Earliest Christianity* (Mifflintown: Sigler, 1996).

[2] See Jennifer Kolpacoff Deane, *A History of Medieval Heresy and Inquisition* (Lanham: Rowman and Littlefield, 2011), and Diarmaid MacCulloch, *The Reformation: A History* (New York: Penguin, 2005) for further details on these heresies.

[3] For a general history of Waldensianism, see Marina Beneddetti, ed., *Storia del Cristianesimo*, vol. 1, *L'età medievale (secoli VIII–XV)* (Rome: Carocci, 2015); Gabriel Audisio, *The Waldensian Dissent: Persecution and Survival, c. 1170–c. 1570*, trans. Claire Davidson (Cambridge: Cambridge University Press, 1999); Giorgio Tourn, *Les Vaudois: L'étonnante aventure d'un peuple-église (1170–1999)* (Turin: Claudiana, 1999); Jean-Jacques Parander, *Abrégé de l'histoire des Vaudois, depuis les temps les plus reculés jusqu'à l'an 1871* (Rome: H. Loescher, 1872); Alexis Muston, *The Israel of the Alps: A Complete History of the Waldenses and Their Colonies, Prepared in Great Part from Unpublished Documents* [1875], trans. John Montgomery (London: Blackie; New York: A.M.S. Press, 1978).

[4] They were named "Waldensians" officially following the death of Vaudès around 1217.

[5] His notice at the Bibliothèque nationale de France references his various other names: Valdès, Pierre Valdo, Valdesius, Pierre Valdès, Pierre de Vaux, Pierre Valdo, Pierre de Vaux, Petrus Valdesius: http://data.bnf.fr/10336669/valdo/#author.other_forms.

until the fourteenth century, almost 150 years after his death, that he is called "Pierre" for the first time in documents. The "Profession of Faith of Valdo" (1180), notably, begins with "que tout fidèle sache que *moi Valdo* et tous mes frères en présence des très saints Évangiles déclarons croire de tout cœur" (may every faithful know that *I, Valdo,* and all my brothers, in the presence of the most holy Gospels wholeheartedly proclaim that we believe).[6] Bernard Gui, the famous inquisitor who prosecuted many Waldensians, refers to them as being born in Lyons: "cujus actor et inventor fuit quidam civis Lugdunensis, nomine Valdesius seu Valdensis, a quo sectatores ejus fuerunt taliter nominate" (It was initiated by a citizen of Lyons called Waldes or Waldo, whose followers took their names from his).[7] These different names are all acceptable denominations and have been widely and interchangeably used in Waldensian scholarship. However, for this book, I will only use "Vaudès" to refer to the father of Waldensianism, following the decision made by Gabriel Audisio.[8]

Vaudès was a rich merchant in twelfth-century Lyons. However, following the example of the *Life of Saint-Alexis*, he became convinced that he had to commit his life to serving God.[9] He immediately sold his possessions and made sure that his wife and his family received a good share of the money. He then decided to start a new life, entirely devoted to poverty and absolute obedience to the scriptures. Unlike Alexis, however, he considered that his pious way of life had to be shared with as many people as possible. Vaudès rapidly found followers, originally only in Lyons. However, his model of humility, devotion, and prayer became popular, as more and more outsiders came to join the nascent community. Even though he was the founder of this movement, he did not consider himself a leader, but merely a guide. With the influx of new converts, Vaudès

---

[6] Tourn, *Les Vaudois*, 229. Italics mine.

[7] Bernard Gui, *Manuel de l'inquisiteur*, ed. and trans. G. Mollat (Paris: Honoré Champion, 1926), 1:34. For the translation, see Janet Shirley, trans., *The Inquisitor's Guide: A Medieval Manual on Heretics* (Welwyn Garden City: Ravenhall Books, 2006), 49.

[8] Gabriel Audisio, one of the most renowned specialists of the movement, decided to use this term in a move that has become the norm for recent scholarship on the subject. See *Waldensian Dissent*, 8–9.

[9] The *Life of Saint-Alexis* is a hagiographic poem, one of the oldest in the vernacular (the oldest versions date from the eleventh century) that relates the life of Alexius of Rome. The son of a wealthy family, he decided to devote his life to God and prayer, and thus gave away all his riches and possessions before fleeing. Disguised as a beggar, he traveled throughout the Roman Empire, first to Edessa, then Rome, always hiding in order to pray. He spent most of his remaining days praying, hidden under a staircase. After his death, his family found him holding a parchment containing a narration of his life devoted to God. See Maurizio Perugi, ed., *La Vie de Saint Alexis* (Geneva: Droz, 2000). Saints' lives were very popular in the Middle Ages, and the *Vie de Saint Alexis* was one of the most famous and most popular at the time.

became aware that his movement might draw the ire of the pope. Even though the early Waldensians considered themselves to be obedient to Rome, the Vatican was still circumspect about their actions, and specifically about the fact that they were preaching without being ordained ministers. But Vaudès still wanted to show the purity of his intentions. Walter Map, the twelfth-century writer, explains in his *De Nugis Curialium* (*Courtier's Trifles*) that he was present when Vaudès and his followers requested an audience with Pope Alexander III during the Third Lateran Council in 1179. They had made the long trip from Lyons in order to defend their right to preach. Map was charged with their interrogation; however, the whole Roman assembly threw them out and mocked them, taking them for fools.[10] Year after year, the movement organized itself more as more people joined it. Two main precepts were at its core. First, in concordance with the original ideals of Vaudès, those who decided to join the movement had to literally abandon everything. Complete deprivation was the only means to truly embrace their objective of adoration and obedience. Bernard Gui was impressed by their desire to rid themselves of everything: "qui dives rubis extitit et relictis omnibus proposuit servare paupertatem et perfectionem evangelicam sicut apostolic servaverunt" ([Vaudès] was rich, but after he gave up all his belongings, he wished to embrace poverty and evangelical perfection, like the apostles did).[11] To offer visual evidence of their commitment, they wore the most modest garb possible, a gunny robe. This fashion choice was a way for them to wear their poverty. It was also a statement for the whole world to see and an important part of their personality. Map explains, "Hii certa nusquam habent domicilia, bini et bini circuent nudi pedes, laneis induti, nichil habentes, omnia sibi communia tanquam apostoli" (These people have no settled abodes; they go about two and two, barefoot, clad in woolen, owning nothing, but having all things in common, as the apostles).[12] Preaching was the other backbone of the movement. The Waldensians firmly believed that all should be able to preach, regardless of intellectual, societal, gender, or religious status. It is probably on this point that the church felt threatened. Because they all could preach, they were all direct actors of their faith and of their relation to God. The traditional Christian system, with a group (the clergy) teaching the word of God to an attentive group of believers, was disrupted in favor of a more direct one, in which every believer was a witness who was to spread the word of God.[13]

---

[10] See Walter Map, *De Nugis Curialium / Courtiers' Trifles*, ed. and trans. M. R. James (Oxford: Clarendon Press, 1983). The passage on Vaudès is chapter 31, "De secta Valdesiorium / Of the Sect of the Waldensians," pp. 124–29.

[11] Gui, *Manuel*, 34.

[12] Map, *De Nugis Curialium*, 126; trans. 127.

[13] See Mark 16:20, "And they went out and preached everywhere, the Lord working with them and confirming the word through the accompanying signs."

In 1180, Vaudès delivered his profession of faith to Cardinal Henry of Clairvaux. The cardinal had been sent to him by the pope, who wanted to assess whether the movement was a threat.[14] This document is of tremendous importance to understand that Vaudès saw the Poor as a movement that respected Rome; he, for instance, had only contempt for the Cathars.[15] Vaudès explains some of the most important precepts of his group. First, the Waldensians, in the profession of faith, recognized the humanity of Christ: "en lui deux natures existent ensemble, c'est à dire Dieu et l'homme en une seule personne. . . . Il a mangé, bu, dormi, s'est fatigué et reposé" (in him two natures coexist together, namely God and man in a single person. . . . He ate, drank, slept, got tired, and took some rest).[16] They hailed the church as "catholique, sainte, apostolique et immaculée, hors de laquelle personne ne peut être sauvé, et les sacrements qui sont administrés en elle sont légitimes" (Catholic, holy, apostolic, and immaculate, outside of which there is no salvation, and the sacraments it delivers are legitimate).[17] One major difference, however, was their rejection of the clergy as a mediator between man and God. They considered the scriptures to be the only guide to follow: "notre intention est de vivre les conseils évangéliques comme étant des precepts impératifs" (it is our intent to follow evangelical advice, as they are imperative precepts).[18] The idea of clergy itself is absent from Waldensian theology. Since all could pray, titular figures like clergymen were not needed. One year later, the late pope Alexander II was replaced by Lucius III, who had more extreme views on the subject. He convoked the Synod of Verona in 1184, during which "Ad abolendam diversam haeresium pravitatem" (On the abolition of some evil heresies) was issued.[19] For the first time, the Poor were condemned as heretics, alongside a few other movements (the Cathars, the Patarines, the Josephites, and the Arnoldists). They all were sentenced to be hunted down and "perpetually banished": "Imprimis ergo Catharos et Patarinos et eos, qui se Humiliatos vel Pauperes de Ludguno falso nomine mentiuntur, Passaginos, Iosephinos, Arnaldistas perpetuo decernimus anathemati subiacere" (More particularly we declare all Cathars, Patarines, and those who call themselves the Humbled, or Poor of Lyons, Passagines, Josephines, Arnoldists, to lie under a perpetual anathema). Every member of society is encouraged to help the church in the hunt for heretics:

---

[14] I am going to use the translation of Biblioteca Nacional de Madrid, MS 1114, present in the appendix of Tourn, *Les Vaudois*, 229–30.

[15] See Audisio, *Waldensian Dissent*, 14.

[16] Tourn, *Les Vaudois*, 230.

[17] Tourn, *Les Vaudois*, 230. This quotes almost perfectly the Nicene Creed ("Et unam, sanctam, catholicam et apostolicam Ecclesiam").

[18] Tourn, *Les Vaudois*, 230.

[19] Later added to Lateran IV as Canon 3.

Sane praedictam excommunicationis sententiam, cui omnes haereticos praecipimus subiacere, ab omnibus patriarchis, archiepiscopis et episcopis in praecipuis festivitatibus, et quoties solennitates habuerint vel quamlibet occasionem, ad gloriam Dei et reprehensionem haereticae pravitatis decernimus innovari, auctoritate apostolica statuentes, ut, si quis de ordine episcoporum in his negligens fuerit vel desidiosus inventus, per triennale spatium ab episcopali habeatur dignitate et administratione suspensus.

[And we further decree, that this excommunication, in which our will is, that all heretics be included, be by all Patriarchs, Archbishops, and Bishops, renewed and repeated in all the chief festivals, and on any public solemnity, or upon any other occasion, to the glory of God, and the putting a stop to all heretical pravity; ordering by our apostolical authority, that if any Bishop be found wanting or slow herein, he be suspended for three years from his episcopal dignity and administration.][20]

The Waldensians were cornered. Lyons, once a refuge, ceased being a haven for them. They were forced into exile, as they were expelled from the city in 1182; fleeing was the only solution. The creation of the Inquisition in 1231, tasked with hunting down and destroying schismatics and heretics, would make it even harder for them to exist as a group. Thus, the community spread out very quickly, throughout France (Roussillon, Provence, Dauphiné, Lorraine) as well as abroad (Italy, principally the Piedmont; Hungary, Bohemia, Bavaria). The concealment of their faith enabled the safeguard of the movement until it became part of the Reformation many years later.

The Waldensians were not deterred by the bull. Claude de Seyssel (1450–1520) was tasked by Rome with collecting evidence against them in the valleys of Piedmont and in the Luberon, in order to mount a solid case for prosecution. Seyssel visited many Waldensian villages in order to understand their faith and precepts. In 1520 he published *Adversus errores et sectam Valdensium disputationes* (Disputation against the errors and the cult of the Waldensians) in which he compiled all their actions and elements of their faith that were punishable.[21] He compiled thirty-eight reprehensible points on their faith, thereby shedding light

---

[20] See *Documenta Catholica Omnia*, http://www.documentacatholicaomnia.eu/04z/ z_1184–11–04__SS_Lucius_III__Ad_Abolendam_Diversam_Haeresium_Pravitatem __LT.doc.html. For the English translation, see http://professor-moriarty.com/info/ files/resources/verona1184.txt.

[21] The text of Seyssel was republished in the seventeenth century, as a dissertation, entitled *La Doctrine de Vaudois, dressée par Claude Seyssel et Claude Coussart, avec notes dressées par Jean Capel* (Sedan, 1618). I am using here the reproduction of the third chapter, "Discours des Vaudois," and of the fourth, "Ce que Seissel reprend aux Vaudois" as they are presented in Samuel Berthalon and Jean-Pierre Muret, eds., *La Doctrine des Vaudois* (Lauris: Éditions du Luberon, 1997). Every quotation comes from this edition (hereafter "Seyssel").

on Waldensian faith." His findings cover the relation to God, the organization of religion, as well as the customs of the Waldensians as a group. The first four points explain how they do not recognize any authority except that of the Bible. Every single one of their actions will only rely on it: "Ils reçoivent . . . seulement ce qui est escrit tant au vieil qu'au nouveau testament" (they only accept the writings of the Old and the New Testament).[22] Interpreting the Bible is impious; as the word of God, the Bible is perfect. Seyssel notes that Waldensians believe that all the writings and glosses produced throughout the centuries have spoiled the holiness of the scriptures: "ils disent que les pontifes romains et les prestres ont depravé l'Escriture par leurs doctrines et leurs gloses" (They say that the Roman pontiffs and the priests have depraved the scriptures with all their doctrines and glosses).[23] Points 8, 9, and 18 cover indulgences and denounce them as an offense to God.[24] Generally, the main problem that separates the Catholic Church and the Waldensians is the role and power of religious institutions. Waldensians considered the church to be corrupt: "Ils disent qu'eux seuls gardent la doctrine Evangelique et Apostolique, et qu'à ceste occasion avec une impudence intolerable ils usurpent le nom d'Eglise Catholique" (They say that only they are the keepers of the evangelical and apostolical doctrine, and thence the clergy usurps with intolerable impudence the name of the Catholic Church).[25] Long before the reformists considered that they were the only legitimate representatives of God on Earth, this idea was already thriving in Waldensian theology.

Seyssel also points to customs that did not infringe on orthodoxy. First, giving money to the church is proscribed for Waldensians; Seyssel notes that even taxes traditionally due to the church were considered sacrilegious: "Ils disent qu'ils ne doivent disme ny premices aux Ecclésiatiques" (They say that they owe neither the tithe nor their first harvest to the ecclesiastics).[26] On par with the attack on the riches of the church, Seyssel also notes that Waldensians do not celebrate saints' days, because only Christ should be adored: "Ils disent que les hommes mortels n'ont point besoin du suffrage des saints, Christ suffisant abondament en toutes choses" (They say that mortal men do not need the help

---

[22] Seyssel, 65.

[23] Seyssel, 66.

[24] "Ils affirment que tout ce que l'on employe pour délivrer des peines de Purgatoire les âmes des trespassés est inutile, perdu, superstitieux" (Seyssel, 69) (They affirm than any action directed at freeing the souls of the dead from the sufferings in Purgatory is useless, damned, superstitious); "Ils disent que nos prestres n'ont aucune puissance de remettre les peschez" (70) (They say that our priests have no power to remit sins); "Ils affirment que les indulgences octroiées par l'Église sont à mespriser" (75) (They argue that the indulgences given by the church should be despised).

[25] Seyssel, 70.

[26] Seyssel, 66.

of saints, for Christ abundantly suffices in all matters).[27] Their dogma is solely based on the scriptures and therefore excludes many concepts of Catholicism that are not directly present in the Bible. Likewise, prayer should not be directed to anyone but God;[28] no food can be consumed before it is blessed.[29] Surprisingly, Seyssel does not condemn their view on transubstantiation; it is present in the Bible,[30] so it seems that it would be accepted by the Waldensians. If no texts from the French branch question this idea, the Lombard and Italian branches, however, were not completely in agreement with their counterparts and were opposed to some of their beliefs.[31]

As the Reformation was settling in Europe, Waldensians became aware of movements with principles close to theirs. After persecutions had intensified, Waldensians and reformists (both Lutherans and Calvinists) had been targeted together as movements to be eliminated. It was decided that unity was the best way to survive the persecutions of the church. In 1532, during the Synod of Chanforan, in Angrogna (Piedmont), the Waldensians officially joined the Reformation. During the late fifteenth century and early sixteenth century, the migratory nature of Waldensianism put the different branches in contact with each other, as well as with the nascent movements of the Reformation. The *barbes*, these itinerant preachers that were crucial to the dissemination of the Waldensian creed, were also fundamental in keeping contact with the different communities that composed the Waldensian diaspora, which had spread across Europe after they were expelled from Lyons. Indeed, the rise of Calvinist and Lutheran ideas throughout Europe helped the Waldensians realize that they

---

[27] Seyssel, 67–68.

[28] "En toute l'Escriture nous n'avons aucune priere qu'a Dieu, dont s'ensuit que les preieres addressées aux Anges ou aux Saints n'ont aucun modele, ni fondement en l'Escriture" (Seyssel, 73) (in the scriptures there are no other prayers but to God, and thus the prayers directed to the angels or to the saints have no model or justification in the scriptures).

[29] Seyssel, 74: "Christ n'a-t-il pas beni le pain au desert?"; Did not Christ bless bread in the desert?).

[30] See Matt. 26:26–28: "And as they were eating, Jesus took bread, blessed and broke it, and gave it to the disciples and said, 'Take, eat; this is My body.' / Then He took the cup, and gave thanks, and gave it to them, saying, 'Drink from it, all of you. / For this is My blood of the new covenant, which is shed for many for the remission of sins'"; Mark 14:22–23: "And as they were eating, Jesus took bread, blessed and broke it, and gave it to them and said, 'Take, eat; this is My body.' / Then He took the cup, and when He had given thanks He gave it to them, and they all drank from it." Luke 22:19–20: "And He took bread, gave thanks and broke it, and gave it to them, saying, 'This is My body which is given for you; do this in remembrance of Me.' / Likewise He also took the cup after supper, saying, 'This cup is the new covenant in My blood, which is shed for you.'"

[31] See Euan Cameron, *Waldenses: Rejections of Holy Church in Medieval Europe* (Oxford: Blackwell, 2000), especially section 3.5, "The Conference of Bergamo" (43–45).

shared multiple beliefs with them. Pope Clement VII had condemned both the Lutherans and the Waldensians and had commissioned Thomas Illyricus the inquisitor in Savoy, tasked with the elimination of the heresies.[32] Gabriel Audisio argues that the contacts between Waldensians and reformists can be traced to the early 1520s, with 1523 the earliest appeal by Martin Luther himself to the Duke of Savoy to protect the Waldensian populations on his lands.[33] During the annual synods that brought together the *barbes*, the struggle of the reformists had been regularly mentioned, and contacts began to be instituted between them. Unifying the movements started to be seen as an eventuality, and even as a necessity in order to survive. Following the 1530 Synod of Mérindol, two *barbes* who spoke Latin (the only language that would make it possible to communicate with the diverse branches), Pierre Masson and Georges Morel, were sent to discuss joining the nascent Reformation. Demands and explanations proliferated on both sides.[34] Twenty-three points were drafted; concessions and changes were made that altered the face of Waldensianism.

The synod in Chanforan not only unified the movements; it also created a solid, common ground that was aimed at facilitating the mutual interactions of the two groups. Some of the core beliefs and precepts of Waldensians, already present in *The Noble Lesson* or in Seyssel's testimony,[35] were reinforced.[36] It was decreed that God was the only entity that should be obeyed: "Nulla opera he quiamata bona si non quella che Dio ha comandata" (No action can be deemed good unless it was ordered by God).[37] Only God could pardon sins; the clergy was once more rebuked: "La confessione aurculare non he commandata da Dio" (the auricular confession is not commanded by God).[38] As Seyssel stated, marriage was an institution that could not be refused to anyone: "El matrimonio non he prohibito ha alcuno de quallunque stato ho ordine che sia" (Marriage is not forbidden to anyone of whatever order or state), thus stating that the celibacy of

---

[32] See M. F. Godefroy, "Vers la frontière: Thomas Illyricus," in *Les Frontières religieuses en Europe du XVe au XVIIe siècle: Actes du XXXIe Colloque international d'études humanistes*, ed. Robert Sauzet (Paris: Librairie Philosophique J. Vril, 2002), 89–96. For the original text of Clement VII's condemnation of the Waldensians and Lutherans, see Luke Wadding, *Scriptores Ordinis Minores* (Rome: Novissima, 1936), 771–78.

[33] See Gabriel Audisio, "Une Mutation: Les vaudois passent à la Réforme (1530–1532)," *Bulletin de la Société de l'Histoire du Protestantisme Français* 126 (1980): 153–65.

[34] See Audisio, *Waldensian Dissent*, 166–69.

[35] The anonymous *La Noble leyçon* (*The Noble Lesson*) is both a summary of the Bible and a list of precepts to be followed. Its origin is unclear (twelfth–fourteenth century); it was highly considered by Waldensians as a very important moral guide.

[36] I will be using the text of the synod as it is presented by Jean Jalla in the "Bollettino Commemorativo del Sinodo di Cianforan (Angrogna), 1532–1932," *Societa di Storia Valdese* 58 (1932): 34–48 (hereafter "Chanforan").

[37] Chanforan, 44.

[38] Chanforan, 45.

priests was not required. Finally, vengeance and violence were still acknowledged as horrible actions that had to be forbidden at all costs: "non he lecito al christiano vindicarsi del suo inimico in sorte nulla que sia" (it is not licit for Christians to take revenge on their enemies in any form it may be).[39]

If Chanforan marked a decisive turn in the recognition of the Waldensian faith among other reformist churches, it is also because changes were made that brought Waldensian doctrine in line with that accepted by Lutherans and Calvinists. Whereas predestination had never been a great issue among Waldensians, it became a point of contention that was finally accepted. Points 19 to 21 underline the importance and irrevocability of predestination:

> Tuti quelli che sono stati et serano salvati sono preelleti avanti la costitutione del mondo. . . . Quelli che sono salvati non posseno essere non salvati. . . . Quicunque statuisse elibero arbitrio denegua in tuto la predestinatione et la gratia de Dio.

> [All those who were and will be saved are preelected before the constitution of the world. . . . Those who have been saved cannot be unsaved. . . . Whoever believes in free will denies predestination and the grace of God.][40]

Predestination had notably been absent from previous texts. What is striking is that poverty, which had been for centuries the foundational base of Waldensianism, was abandoned. Point 23 states, "havere li ministri per nutrire la sua familha qualque cosa in particulare non he contra la comunione apostolica" (For a minister, possessing goods in order to provide for his family is not against the apostolic communion[41]). This dramatic change in their dogma was also accompanied by a drastic redevelopment of the place of their beliefs in their everyday life.

The faith of the Waldensians evolved, but it was always, from its origins to the sixteenth century, condemned by Rome. In spite of all the changes to its original core beliefs, this highly religious group never compromised or stopped believing. Despite the best efforts of the royal troops, the massacres of the Luberon did not put an end to almost five hundred years of religious history. If the communities in France suffered a terrible blow, Waldensians survived the wars and inspired other reform movements.

---

[39] Chanforan, 46.
[40] Chanforan, 47.
[41] Chanforan, 47.

# The Waldensians in Provence:
## Origins and History

After their expulsion from Lyons, the Waldensians migrated to the Italian Alps, the Piedmont, and Bohemia. The great plague epidemic of the fourteenth century (1346–57) indirectly provided them an opportunity to settle in France again. The death toll was catastrophic throughout Europe. Gabriel Audisio traces the settlement of Waldensians in the Luberon during the fifteenth century, particularly in the Comtat Venessin,[1] a papal state located just outside of Avignon and centered around the municipality of Carpentras.[2] Faced with a drastic lack of workers, the administrators of the Comtat amended its status in order to attract newcomers. Any foreigner who chose to settle there was guaranteed a ten-year tax exemption.[3] This brought a great Waldensian diaspora to the region from the Piedmontese Alps; they came and started working for rich Catholic landowners. The Waldensians were known as gifted laborers who produced miracles on hard-to-work soils, which they made flourish.[4]

In spite of their impact on the economy, the Waldensians were the targets of attacks, which culminated with the massacres in 1545. The Reformation greatly accelerated their demise. Francis I, king of France (1494–1547), was originally indifferent, if not tolerant, to the reformist movements that were burgeoning

---

[1] The department of Vaucluse is composed of most of the territories that once formed the Comtat.

[2] Gabriel Audisio, in *Les Vaudois du Luberon: Une minorité en Provence (1460–1560)* (Gap: Association d'études vaudoises et historiques du Luberon, 1984), 45–49, presents an extremely detailed analysis of the different migration flows that brought the Waldensians to settle in Provence.

[3] Audisio notes article 158 of the statutes of the Comtat: "Que soient octroyez franchises libertéz et immunités à tous ceux, qui de dehors viendront pour voir fare continuelle demeurance et perpétuelle aux lieus de la Comté de Venaiscin, qu'ilz ne soient tenus à contribution de charges quelconques pendant l'epace ou le temps de dix ans." (*Vaudois du Lubéron*, 68–69). For other accounts on the settlement, see by the same author *Une Grande migration alpine en Provence (1460–1560)* (Turin: Deputazione subalpina di storia patria, 1989) and *Migranti valdesi, Delfinato, Piemonte, Provenza (1460–1560) – Migrants vaudois, Dauphiné, Piémont, Provence* (Turin: Claudiana, 2011).

[4] See notably chap. 7, "The Southwestern Alps," in Euan Cameron, *Waldenses: Rejections of Holy Church in Medieval Europe* (Oxford: Blackwell, 2000), 151–208.

in his kingdom. However, his point of view changed drastically following the infamous Affair of the Placards. During the night of October 17, 1534, many Protestant *placards* (flyers, posters) were nailed on the doors and walls of different public places, one of them on the door of the king's bedroom in the royal castle of Amboise. Entitled "Articles véritables sur les horribles, grands et insupportables abus de la messe papale, inventée directement contre la sainte cène de notre Seigneur, seul Médiateur et seul Sauveur Jésus Christ" (True articles on the horrible, great, and unbearable excesses of the papal mass, directly invented in opposition to the holy Last Supper of our Lord, sole intermediary and savior Jesus Christ), they were authored by Antoine Marcourt, who lived in Neuchatel, Switzerland, at the time.[5] The placards violently targeted the church, and specifically the pope, whose actions were seen as catastrophic; the pamphlet claimed that the world "sera totalement ruiné, abîmé, perdu et désolé" (will be completely ruined, lost, and desolated) because of him.[6]

The king was furious after the widespread and targeted posting of the placards; he perceived this event as a plot to destroy the French monarchy. As a consequence, he quickly passed an edict condemning heresy on January 29, 1535:

> François, etc. sçavoir faisons que pour la conservation et augmentation de la foy catholique, extirpation et éradication de la secte luthérienne, et autres hérésies . . . dont les sectateurs et imitateurs se sont rendus fugitifs, cachent et latitent en aucunes parties de nostre royaume où ils sont tenus et supportez par aucuns de noz sujets qui les récèlent, pour empescher qu'ils ne soient punis par justice, nous avons statué et ordonné . . . que tous ceux et celles qui ont recélé ou recéleront par cy-après scientement lesdits sectateurs, pour empescher qu'ils ne fussent pris et apprehendez par la justice, et qui pour raison dudit cas seront absentez et renduz fugitifs . . . seront punis de telle et semblable peine que lesdits sectateurs.[7]

> [Frenchmen, etc. We let you know that, for the conservation and growth of the Catholic faith, and in order to eradicate and exterminate the Lutheran doctrine, and other heresies . . . whose disciples and imitators have become fugitives, hidden everywhere in our kingdom, where they are supported and sustained by some of our subjects who conceal them, so that they are

---

[5] He was the author of a *Petit traité . . . de la Sainte Eucharistie* (*Small treatise . . . on the Holy Eucharist*) in whose preface he states quite explicitly that he alone could not have distributed the placards. It seems that they were smuggled into France by Guillaume Feret, a servant of the king's apothecary, and put up in Paris by a group of radical dissenters." R. J. Knecht, *Francis I* (Cambridge: Cambridge University Press, 1982), 249.

[6] The text of the pamphlet can be found on the website of the Musée virtuel du Protestantisme français: https://www.museeprotestant.org/wp-content/uploads/2014/01/Mus%C3%A9e-virtuel-du-protestantisme-Les-placards-contre-la-messe-1534.pdf.

[7] Eugène Haag and Emile Haag, *La France protestante ou vie des protestants français qui se sont faits un nom dans l'Histoire. Pièces justificatives* (Paris: Joël Cherbulier, 1858), 6.

not punished by justice, we have decreed and ordered that . . . all those, men
or women, who have deliberately hidden, or who will hide those disciples,
to prevent them from being arrested and apprehended, and who, for this
reason, will be absent and fugitive . . . will be punished with the same sentence as the said disciples.]

The edict clearly states that heretics and their "friends" will not be tolerated any
longer in the kingdom and will be eliminated; the apposition at the very beginning of "François" (Frenchmen) shows that heretics were considered by the king
to not be French, and thus were de facto enemies of the Crown. However, with
the signature of patent letters on July 16, 1535, in Coucy (now known as the
Edict of Coucy), the king seemingly calmed his stance. Long presented as an
edict of toleration and forgiveness, its message is nevertheless far from charitable.
It explains that those of the new religion who will accept to abjure it would be
pardoned and recognized as true Christians:

> ains en soy retournant vers luy et sa bonté infinite, luy ont demandé grace
> et miséricorde, et ont fait penitence publique, en repentance de leursdictes
> erreurs, et sont morts comme bons chrétiens et catholiques, à la louange de
> Dieu et exaltation de son église.

> [thus, turning back toward him and his infinite kindness, begged him for
> grace and mercy, and made public penance, repenting for their mistakes,
> and died as good Christians and Catholics, praising God and exalting his
> church.]

The heretics are portrayed as evil in the edict: "les hérésies et sectes nouvelles,
contraires et desrogantes à la saincte foy et loy catholique de son église, constitution et tradition d'icelle" (the new heresies and cults, opposed to the precepts and
denying the holy faith and Catholic law, with its Church, its constitution, and
its tradition).[8]

The Protestants are accused of heresy; repression was therefore the only
possible answer. Their punishment will be swift and severe: "ilz seront puigniz
estroictement et griefvement, sellon l'exigence du cas" (they will be punished
violently and harshly, as their case necessitates). As he was the arm of God, the
king would thus execute the punishment: "il nous est possible, nous conformer
à sa voullanté, et user de grace et misericorde pour la peine corporelle et tempo-
relle, ainsi qu'il luy plaist faire pour la peine éternelle" (it is our duty to conform

---

[8] *Bulletin du Comité des travaux historiques et scientifiques, section d'histoire et de philologie,* vols. 3–4 (Paris: Imprimerie Nationale, 1885), 223. All the letters and edicts of
Francis I come from this volume. The fact that there is a reference to their death here ("et
sont morts comme bons chrétiens et catholiques") leads us to believe that their conversion
happened on the stake.

ourselves to his will, and to use grace and mercy for corporal and temporal punishment, just as it pleases him to use the eternal punishment). Pardon would be granted only to those who willfully abjured. However, it had to be done within six months: "ilz seront tenus abjurer canoniquement dedans six moys prochains venans" (they will be forced to abjure canonically within the next six months).[9] The leniency of the king is a mere ultimatum. His message is completely unambiguous: abide by my rule or, after six months, you will be hunted down and destroyed. What about the Waldensians? These letters were not directly targeting them. However, since they were a heresy denounced by Rome, they were also targeted, even though they had nothing to do with the placards. In the "Lettres déclaratoires au sujet des lettres précédentes" from September 15, 1535, a few weeks after the Edict of Coucy, Francis reaffirms that Provence is an important part of the kingdom, over which he has power, as he explains at the very beginning of the document: "Françoys, par la grace de Dieu, roy de France, comte de Provence, Forcalquier et terres adjacentes, à nos amez et féaulx conseillers les gens de nostre court de parlement de Prouvence" (Francis, by the grace of God, king of France, count of Provence, Forcalquier,[10] and adjacent lands, to our beloved and trustworthy counselors and people of our court in the Parliament of Provence). The king points out that he is the only authority of the kingdom, after God, and his decisions do not need to be explained and cannot be discussed, "car tel est nostre plaisir, nonobstant quelzconques ordonnances, restrinctions, mandemens ou défences à ce contraires" (for such is our pleasure, regardless of any ordinance, restriction, orders, bans that may arise).[11] His word is final, and whatever he wishes will happen, even in a part of the kingdom that benefited from large exceptions like Provence.

Provence became a part of the kingdom after its annexation in 1481; however, it still had a parliament that enabled the province to have extensive legislative powers. The Waldensian population of the Luberon was targeted by many judicial decisions, as narrated in *Histoire mémorable de la persecution et saccagement du peuple de Merindol & Cabrieres & d'autres circonvoisins, appelez Vaudois* (1555), attributed to Jean Crépin. The *Histoire mémorable* particularly traces the massacres of Cabrières and Mérindol back to one of these events. Collin Pellenc, a Waldensian, was summoned to Aix and subsequently burned on the pyre in 1540

---

[9] *Bulletin*, 225.

[10] The county of Forcalquier used to be independant from Provence, until the thirteenth century, when both were united. The village of Forcalquier is located in the Alpes-de-Haute-Provence department in France, approximately forty miles east of Cabrières-d'Avignon.

[11] *Bulletin*, 225.

# The Waldensians in Provence

in Aix-en-Provence, on the ground of heresy.[12] Other people were later summoned in court; a group of men from the region of Cabrières, "André Mainard, Iēa [Jean] Cabrie, François Mainard, dict Chaiz, Iean Bony, Antoine Palenq, Guillaume Armant, Michel Mainard, Iēa Palenq, Mondon Brunerol, Faci Bernard," decided to go the tribunal, since they did not expect to risk anything but still wanted to defend their right to practice their religion. However, when they arrived in Aix, they were informed by their lawyers that they had been explicitly ordered to not defend them. One of the attorneys even announced that they were facing many dangers:

> Toutesfois, l'un des advocats leur dit secrettement & à part, qu'ils ne se devoyent presenter à ladicte Cour, sinon qu'ils fussent prests & appareillez de endurer d'estre bruslez et fricassez à petit feu,[13] & feu de paille, sans autre forme ne figure de proces. Car cela estoit dejia par ladicte Cour conclue & arresté côtre eux.[14]

> [However, one of the lawyers secretly took them aside and told them in private that they should not present themselves to the court, unless they were ready and prepared to endure to be burned alive and slowly, without any kind of trial. For the court had already convened and made its decision.]

The Waldensians decided not to go to court, for fear that they would face the same fate as Pellenc.[15] The parliament took notice of their decision and used this occasion to craft the document that would eventually lead to the attacks in the Luberon.

The Judgment of Mérindol followed the Waldensians' absence in court. It denounces the extreme gravity of their heresy, described as a "crime de lèse-

---

[12] See Gabriel Audisio, *Procès-verbal d'un massacre: Les Vaudois du Lubéron (avril 1545)* (Aix-en-Provence: EDISUD, 1992), 17–22. Louis Serre and Jacques Pellenc, who were accompanying him, were also sentenced to death.

[13] Slowly roasting people made their agony longer. See notably John Foxe, *Foxe's Book of Martyrs: A Complete and Authentic Account of the Lives, Sufferings, and Triumphant Deaths of the Primitive and Protestant Martyrs in All Parts of the World, with Notes, Comments and Illustrations*, ed. John Milner and Ingram Cobin (London: Knight and Son, 1856).

[14] Jean Crespin, *Histoire mémorable de la persécution et saccagement du peuple de Merindol et Cabrières et autre circon-voisins, appelez Vaudois* (Geneva, 1556), 1–2.

[15] "Ils virēt devant leurs yeux rigoureusemēt et cruellement tormenter et meurtrir plusieurs bōs personnages, n'ayans autre cause en leur condamnation, sinon qu'ils avoyent dict & maintenu propos, qui estpyent declarez Lutheriens par les Docteurs en Theologie" (Crespin, *Histoire mémorable*, 2) (they witnessed, before their eyes, many good people rigorously and cruelly tormented, without being condemned, except that they had confessed and said that they had been recognized as Lutherans by doctors in theology).

majesté divine et humaine" (a crime of divine and human lèse-majesté).[16] The text reminds everybody that in spite of the great kindness of the king, who gave all the heretics six months to convert, the Waldensians were still preaching six years later:

> Le recollement des témoins acaminés et des susdites informations, autres charges et information et proces produits par le susdit procureur general pour faire apparoir que notoirement ceux de Mérindol tiennent sectes vaudoises et luthériennes réprouvées et contraires à la Sainte foi et Religion Chrétienne; scellent et retirent gens étrangers et fugitifs chargés et diffamés d'être de telle secte et iceux entretiennent et favorisent; qu'en lieu il y a école d'erreurs et fausses doctrines des dites sectes; gens qui dogmatisent les dites erreurs et fausses doctrines et ont imprimé et vendent pleins de telles fausses doctrines. Et aussi que ceux de Mérindol au terroir ou au rocher ont bâti des cavernes et spelonques, où ils retirent et cachent eux, leurs complices et leurs biens.[17]

> [The reading of the depositions of the witnesses, of the previous information, as well as other charges, pieces of evidence, and reports produced by the attorney general have notoriously shown that the people of Mérindol host forbidden Lutheran and Waldensian cults, against the holy faith and the Christian religion; they host foreign people and fugitives guilty of belonging to such cults, and they are benevolent with them, and provide them with food and shelter; that there can be found schools teaching the mistakes and false doctrines of these people; there are people who preach such errors and wrong doctrines, and who have printed and sold many of these doctrines. It also proves that those of Mérindol have built, in their territories and in rocks, many caverns and caves, where they are hiding themselves, their goods, and their accomplices.]

In this excerpt, the Waldensians are also accused of harboring foreign agents, and thus are a menace to law-abiding Catholic subjects of Provence and of the Crown. As a consequence, they must be punished, and are "condamnés . . . à estre brulés et ards tous vifs" (sentenced . . . to be burned alive at the stake). They are not authorized to remain on any land on which the king reigns: "et au regard des femmes, enfants, serviteurs ou famille de tous ces sus défaillants et condamnés, . . . au cas qu'ils ne puissant être pris ou appréhendés dès maintenant les a tous bannis et bannies, du royaume, terre et seigneurerie du roi" (concerning the women, children, servants, and relatives of all these men, sentenced in absentia . . . if they are not captured or arrested now, they will all be banished from the kingdom, the land, and domain of the king). They are forced into exile, and any

---

[16] Jean-Guy Arché, *Le Massacre des Vaudois du Luberon* (Aubenas: Curandera, 1984), 37. The text is reproduced in this book (37–38) and is the version used in this chapter.

[17] Arché, *Le Massacre des Vaudois du Luberon*, 37–38.

attempt to come back to their former land will be met with immediate execution: "avec interdiction et prohibition d'y entrer ni venir sous peine de la hard et du feu" (they are forbidden and prohibited to ever come back, under pain of execution by hanging or burning at the stake).[18]

If the Edict of Coucy was a warning, the Judgment of Mérindol is a bona fide declaration of war, a death sentence for the whole Waldensian population: "la cour a ordonné et ordonne que toutes les maisons et bastides du lieu seront abattues, démolies et abrasées, et le dit lieu sera rendu inhabitable, sans que personne y puisse réédifier, ni bâtir, si ce n'est par le pouvoir et permission du roi" (the court has ordered and orders that all the houses and country houses of that place be knocked down, destroyed, and razed, and said place will be made uninhabitable, and nobody will be able to build or reconstruct anything without the king's permission).[19] Destroying the Waldensians was not without risk for the economy of the whole region. Their importance for the economy of the Luberon, and even Provence, was tremendous. They were employed by nobles and landowners as a cheap laboring force; killing or expelling them would then have dire economic consequences. In spite of this, the march to elimination was already in full gear, and very soon, nothing stood in opposition to its application.

---

[18] Arché, *Le Massacre des Vaudois du Luberon*, 38.

[19] This idea is made really clear in Crespin, *Histoire mémorable*: "Mais aussi par ledict arrest furēt condamnez tous les manans & habitants dudict Merindol . . . à estre tous bruslez, tant hommes que femmes, qu'enfans, sans reserver aucune persone. Et par le mesme Arrest furt dict, que toutes les maisons de Merindol seroient abbatues, & le village du tout raze & deshabité: & de tous les arbres du tout couppez, tant oliviers qu'autres, sans rien laisser, & ce à cinq cens pas à la ronde: tellement que le lieu fut rendu du tout inhabitable." (2–3) (likewise, all the residents and inhabitants of Mérindol . . . were sentenced to be burned alive, men and women, children, without sparing anyone. And in the same edict, it was said that all the houses in Mérindol would be destroyed, and the village razed and emptied: and all the trees will be cut, even the olive trees, without leaving a single one standing, five hundred feet around. As such, the place will be made completely unlivable.) Interestingly, there are few variations between the *Histoire mémorable* and the Judgment. Both emphasize the desolation that will be brought to the villages. The *Histoire mémorable* adds the interesting detail of the olive trees. The Luberon Waldensians were poor peasants, with a very high majority living off manual labor. In Provence, since antiquity, the production and commerce of olives and olive oil was one of the most important resources of the province. This point is present very early in the study of Waldensian history. Already in 1855, Jane Louisa Willyams, in her *A Short History of the Waldensian Church in the Valleys of Piedmont, from the Earliest Period to the Present Time* (London: James Nisbet and Co., 1855), explains about the Waldensians who had settled in Provence that they were people "trained to the laborious toil of the fields, skillful in planting the vine and the olive" (72). Because the Waldensians were highly dependent on agriculture, and particularly oleiculture, destroying the olive trees was a quick way to put their existence to an end.

On January 31, 1545, the order to execute the Waldensians was put into motion and led to the April expeditions. Jacques Meynier d'Opède, president of the Parliament of Provence, was tremendously important in the organization of the attacks. The d'Opèdes were a very old Provençal family, whose power and presence in the region dated centuries back.[20] In 1543, Guillaume Garçonnet, then president of the Parliament of Provence, died. D'Opède, as his second-in-command, became the new president. He is portrayed in every single Protestant source as the evil mastermind behind the massacre. Contrary to his predecessor, d'Opède was much more proactive in his handling of the Waldensian question; Jean Crespin notably describes his zeal to prepare the armies for the expedition: "Iean Minier Sieur Dopede . . . employa tout son credit & toute sa force pour executer non seulemēt le côtenu dudict arrest: mais come vray serviteur & bourreau du diable, encore d'avātage: comme son exploit l'a bien demōstré" (Jean Meynier, Sire of d'Opède . . . used all his credit and strength to execute not only the content of said decision, but, as a true servant and executioner of the Devil, even more, as his actions have shown).[21] A joint army of French and Provençal troops gathered and wiped the region out, destroying village after village. Six hundred men in Cabrières fought against the five thousand soldiers of d'Opède. Seeing that they would likely be massacred, the inhabitants of Cabrières asked the troops to let them go to exile to Germany, with the promise that they would never come back. This was immediately rejected by d'Opède, who, according to the *Histoire mémorable*, wished for their deaths to be as painful and humiliating as possible.[22] Women, including pregnant ones, were locked in a barn that was set ablaze. Those who tried to escape were pierced with pitchforks.[23] All were massacred; children and old people were not spared.[24] How many people died? It is always complicated to assert such a number, because the sources, whether Protestant or Catholic, try to either maximize or minimize the massacre. The *Histoire mémorable* argues that eight hundred children, women, and old people

---

[20] A succinct history of the d'Opède barony can be found in Jean-Anthoine Piton-Curt, *Histoire de la noblesse du comté-Venaissin d'Avignon et de la Principauté d'Orange, dressée sur les preuves, dédiée au Roy*, vol. 1 (Paris: David et Delormel, 1763).

[21] Jean Crespin, *Le Livre des martyrs, qui est un receuil de plusieurs martyrs qui ont endure la mort pour le Nom de nostre Seigneur Iesus Christ, depuis Iēa Hus iusques à ceste anné presente M. D. LIIII* (Geneva, 1554), 662–63.

[22] "Ie les veux prendre tous, sans qu'aucun puisse eschapper de mes mains: et ie les envoyerai habiter au pays d'enfer avec tous les diables, et eux, et leurs femmes et leus enfants" (Crespin, *Histoire Mémorable*, 99) (I want to capture all of them, and that none be able to escape my grip; and I will send them live in the land of hell, with all the devils, and them, their wives, and their children).

[23] Crespin, *Histoire mémorable*, 97.

[24] Crespin, *Histoire mémorable*, 98.

died.[25] For Jean Crespin, it is approximately one thousand people who were executed, also without distinction of sex or age. Those who were not massacred were stripped of all possessions; for fear that they would be punished, they all decided to leave en masse. Six hundred men were sent to the galleys or enslaved. Many more men, women, and children died from the famine that followed.[26]

The Waldensians were wiped out, and their possessions destroyed. However, it was very often the lands of rich Catholic landowners that were ravaged. The "dame du Cental," Mérite de Trivulce, was one of these landowners. She was the wife of Louis de Bouliers, lord of Cental,[27] and daughter of Jacques de Trivulce, a Milanese general who had fought for France at the Battle of Marignano. Jacques Aubéry, who would be the attorney of the Crown in the trial that took place later on, explains how her complaint quickly reached the king: "le roi manda auxdits commissaires, après que la dame de Cental se fut plainte à lui du brûlement et des violences faites en ses terres, qu'ils lui envoyassent leur procès-verbal" (the king asked his officers, after the lady of Cental complained about the fact that her lands were burned down and ransacked, to send him their report).[28] There was simply no other solution for the Crown. Indeed, news of the massacre had quickly spread throughout Europe. The fact that the decision of the king on Cabrières had been botched in such a way—leading to the atrocious massacres in the Luberon—was also another reason for which justice had to be served. The trial, however, also led to a thorny problem: those responsible for mishandling the attacks had to be punished, but without tainting the reputation of the late Francis I and also without giving the impression that they were defending the actions of heretics.

The trial opened on September 18, 1551. In his opening statement, Aubéry explains that if knowing the truce and punishing the culprits was the main reason for the trial, restoring the actions of the late king was also crucial: "la troisième raison est le nom, la mémoire et la reputation du feu roi François, père du roi, auquel semblerait lui être fait tort si par cette plaidoirie publique n'était réparée la plaie que l'on a faite à sa majesté et clémence" (the third reason is the name,

---

[25] "Dont le nombre de ceux qui ont esté si inhumainement meurtris, a esté d'environ huit cens persones, tant hommes que femmes et enfans" (Crespin, *Histoire mémorable*, 98) (the number of those who have been so cruelly bruised was of approximately eight hundred men, women, and children).

[26] Since their lands had been seized or destroyed, and their possessions confiscated, providing food was a real issue, especially since an edict prevented the inhabitants of the adjacent lands from helping the fleeing Waldensians.

[27] For a more detailed history of the Trivulce and Bouliers families, see Robert de Brianson, *L'État et le nobiliaire de Provence* (Paris: Aubin, Emeri, Clousier, 1683), especially 420–30.

[28] Jacques Aubéry, *Histoire de l'éxécution de Cabrières et de Mérindol et d'autres lieux de Provence*, ed. Gabriel Audisio (Paris: Éditions de Paris, 1990), 101.

the memory, and the reputation of late king Francis, father of the king, which reputation should be restored by this public plea, and whose majesty and clemency was wounded).[29] Was Aubéry pro-Waldensian? Not at all. On the contrary, he considered that heretics should be executed and wiped out: "nous devons donc poursuivre les hérétiques . . . comme la vérité poursuit le mensonge" (thus, we must hunt the heretics . . . just like truth hunts down lies).[30] However, the actions of the troops were, according to him, inexcusable: "mais se déchaîner, sans tenir compte du sexe et de l'âge contre une multitude qui n'a pas pu s'exprimer, et qu'on a pas jugé, qui dira que cela est chrétien, sauf celui qui voudra bien reconnaître politiquement qu'il n'est pas chrétien" (but rage, with no consideration whatsoever for age or gender against a multitude who could not speak, and which was not judged, how could anyone argue that this was Christian behavior, except he who will publicly acknowledge that he is not Christian).[31]

Meynier d'Opède, the Catholic leader, was the main defendant. He had strong protectors (notably popes Paul III and Julius III) and was exonerated of any wrongdoing. He was reinstated in 1553, returned to the parliament of Aix the following year, and remained there until his death in 1558. However, a culprit was needed: it was Guillaume Guérin, a lawyer who was sentenced to death for falsification of official documents, an offense that was completely removed from the massacres themselves. D'Opède never had to suffer the consequences of his actions. The events of Cabrières were, then, largely forgotten, judicially speaking, even though they kept on raging in the spirits of those who had been the direct or indirect victims or witnesses of the horrors. But the leniency of the sentence, surprisingly, was also a foundational act for the Waldensian memory. Because such a horror had remained unpunished, the memory of its victims had to remain vivid. The *Tragedy of the Sack of Cabrières*, among other documents, stands as this testimony of their martyrdom, for all to witness and to remember.

---

[29] Aubéry, *Histoire de l'éxécution*, 12.

[30] Aubéry, *Histoire de l'éxécution*, 12.

[31] Aubéry, *Procès verbal*, 7.

# Analyzing *Cabrières*:
# Religion, Community, Violence

The French wars of religion were a series of eight civil wars opposing, throughout the second half of the sixteenth century (1562–98), the Catholics and the Protestants in France over the rights of the latter to freely practice their religion. Only the Edict of Nantes, signed in 1598 by Henri IV, the king of France who converted to Catholicism to become king, granted immunity and authorized them to practice their religion. These wars were bloody, both on the battlefield and as they were represented in literature.[1] Catholics and Protestants produced countless pieces spanning different genres, fueling hatred and resentment. Narratives of massacres developed into poetry, prose, and theater throughout the sixteenth century.[2] Many playwrights, both Catholic and Protestant, used the religious troubles as sources for their tragedies. One can think for instance of *Abraham sacrifiant*, written by the Protestant Théodore de Bèze (1550), or *Les Juifves*, by the very Catholic Robert Garnier (1583), among many others. The religious troubles in France even inspired authors outside the kingdom, like Christopher Marlowe, who retold the events of the Saint Bartholomew's Day massacre in *The Massacre at Paris* (1593).

While medieval theater mostly consisted of farce, morality plays, miracle plays, *sotties*, and mystery plays, Renaissance authors started translating and adapting Latin and Greek authors; this movement eventually led to the development of humanist tragedies based on religious, mythological, or (more rarely)

---

[1] See notably Katherine Maynard and Jeff Kendrick, eds., *Polemic and Literature Surrounding the French Wars of Religion* (Boston: De Gruyter/MIP, 2019); Mack P. Holt, ed., *The French Wars of Religion, 1562–1629* (Cambridge: University of Cambridge Press, 2005); R. J. Knecht, *The French Religious Wars, 1562–1598* (Oxford: Osprey Publishing, 2002); Denis Crouzet, *Dieu en ses royaumes: Une histoire des guerres de religion* (Paris: Champvallon, 2015).

[2] Pierre de Ronsard (in his *Discours*) and Théodore Agrippa d'Aubigné (*Les Tragiques*) wrote poetry about the wars. In his *Histoires prodigieuses les plus mémorables qui ayent esté observées, depuis la Nativité de Iesus Christ, iusques à nostre siècle: Extraites de plusieurs fameux autheurs, Grecz, & Latins, sacrez & profanes* (Paris, 1560), Pierre Boaistuau translated different pieces about monsters and used them in a discussion of the religious troubles. Many plays were produced in this period. See Christian Biet, *Théâtre de la cruauté et récits sanglants en France (XVIe–XVIIe siècles)* (Paris: Laffont, 2006).

contemporary events. In a century that saw a profusion of tragedies, the *Tragedy of the Sack of Cabrières* (hereafter *Cabrières*) stands out as the only play depicting the massacres in Provence of 1545.[3] For a long time it was not given any scholarly attention. Raymond Lebègue, the famous specialist of early modern French theater, did not have much praise for it and instead argued that it was "une pièce de propagande, qu'alourdissent les exposés théologiques" (a propagandist play, coarsened by theological accounts).[4] Charles Mazouer, likewise, discredited it: "il faut cependant mentionner la *Tragédie du sac de Cabrières*, où j'ai personnellement bien du mal à voir un talent de dramaturge" (I must nevertheless mention the *Tragedy of the Sack of Cabrières*, in which I personally barely see any talent in dramaturgy).[5] It is with Timothy Reiss's article "The Origins of French Tragedy" that the play started to receive some recognition: "A play such as the anonymous *Tragédie du sac de Cabrières* (c. 1566), whose chief object was the horror of the Catholic massacre of Cabrières but which gave more space to discussing the power of language, combined these two aims."[6] *Cabrières* is known at least marginally by most sixteenth-century French literature specialists. However, scholarship on the play is meager. Aside from this short allusion by Reiss, there are only four articles that analyze it. Roger Klotz's proposes a close reading of its themes.[7] Olivier Millet establishes how the narratives of both the Waldensians and the Catholics intertwine the narration with truth and lies, which leads to the transformation of the discourse of the different protagonists.[8] Anne Baretaud examines how such plays developed catastrophic events to bring them forward, so that the spectator becomes a witness of such horrors.[9] Finally, I previously discussed how masculinity, governance, and piety are intertwined in the tragedy

---

[3] There are only two other literary narratives on the massacre at Cabrières; Jean Crespin's *Livre des Martyrs* (1554), and *Histoire mémorable de la persécution et saccagement du peuple de Merindol et Cabrières et autre circon-voisins, appelez Vaudois*, also attributed to Crespin. Both are centered around this massacre, its origins, and its aftermath.

[4] Raymond Lebègue, *La Tragédie française de la Renaissance* (Brussels: Office de la Publicité, 1983), 31.

[5] Charles Mazouer, *Le Théâtre français de la Renaissance* (Paris: Honoré Champion, 2002), 238.

[6] Timothy Reiss, "The Origins of French Tragedy," in *A New History of French Literature*, ed. Denis Hollier (Cambridge, MA: Harvard University Press, 1998), 207.

[7] Roger Klotz, "Lecture méthodique de la *Tragédie du sac de Cabrières*," *L'Information Littéraire* 46 (1994): 36–39.

[8] Olivier Millet, "Vérité et mensonge dans la *Tragédie du sac de Cabrières*: Une dramaturgie de la parole en action," *Australian Journal of French Studies* 21, no. 3 (1994): 259–73.

[9] Anne Baretaud, "Le Récit comme acte dans les tragédies bibliques du XVIe siècle," *Loxias* 12 (2006), http://revel.unice.fr/loxias/index.html?id=935.

*Analyzing Cabrières* 23

in order to create fluid communities.[10] This chapter will focus for the most part on three important themes: violence, emotions, and religion. Deploying these themes, I will analyze how history is put into words and disseminated to the audience in *Cabrières*. Andrea Frisch notes that "the intersection of history and tragedy was apparent to the sixteenth-century French, many of whom saw a link between their experiences and the privileged theatrical mode of the ancients."[11] *Cabrières* reproduces history, shaping it to form a representation of truth that fits the codes accepted by its potential audience, while also marking the historical event as particularly significant. This tragedy also stands out among more traditional tragedies; in order to understand its singular place in the history of French tragedy it is important to understand how tragedies were received and understood during the sixteenth century.

## Cabrières' Setting and Form

Tragedies, dating from their Greek and Roman origins, have been codified. Many rules, based on the "ars poetica," rhetorical guides from antiquity, defined tragedies as a theatrical genre. First, the protagonists had to be of high lineage (such as a king, a prince, etc.). Second, tragedies had to be resolved by sadness, death, or destruction. In his *Dictionnarium Latinogallicum* (1543), Robert Estienne defines it as "une sorte d'ancienne moralité ayant les personnages de grans affaires, comme roys, princes, et autres, et dont l'issüe estoit tousjours piteuse" (a sort of ancient morality, with characters of high rank, such as kings, princes, and others, in which the denouement is always piteous).[12] The definition of tragedy by Jacques Peletier du Mans in the *Art poétique français* (1555) is also very close to Estienne's:

> En la tragédie s'introduisent Rois, Princes et grans seigneurs. . . . En la Tragédie, la fin est toujours luctueuse et lamentable ou horrible à voir. Car la matière d'icelle sont occisions, exils, malheureux definements de fortunes, d'enfans et de parents.[13]

> [In tragedies, kings, princes, and great lords are introduced. . . . In tragedies, the end is always pitiful, sorrowful, or horrible to see. Because their matters are bloodbaths, exiles, adverse changes of fortune, death of children and family.]

---

[10] Charles-Louis Morand Métivier, "La Construction de la masculinité dans la *Tragédie du sac de Cabrières*: Le cas d'Opède," *Modern Languages Open* 1, no. 10 (2018): 1–14, doi10.3828/mlo.v0i0.171.

[11] Andrea Frisch, "French Tragedy and the Civil Wars," *Modern Languages Quarterly* 67, no. 3 (2006): 289.

[12] Leblanc, *Les Écrits théoriques*, 48.

[13] Leblanc, *Les Écrits théoriques*, 303.

Renaissance tragedies were also supposed to represent events set in a distant past, either mythological or biblical. Jacques Peletier, for instance, explains that a tragedy must relate to antiquity:

> Si le Français veut ramener les personnes anciennes: qu'il fasse une Niobè triste et désolée, une Médée horrible et affreuse, au Ajax étonné et forcené, un Oreste furieux et vagabond, un Hercule terrible et, comme les latins disent, truculent.[14]

> [If the Frenchman wants to bring back people from antiquity, he should draft a sad and sorry Niobe, a horrible and atrocious Medea, an aghast and raging Ajax, a furious and vagrant Orestes, a belligerent and terrible Hercules, as the Latins say.]

Likewise, Pierre de Ronsard argues in "À Jacques Grévin," an elegy at the beginning of *Le Théâtre de Jacques Grévin* (1562),

> L'argument du Comicque est de toutes saisons,
> Mais celuy du Tragicque est de peu de maisons.
> D'Athenes, Troye, Argos, de Thebes et Mycenes
> Sont pris les arguments qui conviennent aux scenes.[15]

> [The argument of comedies is everyday life,
> But that of tragedies is really constrained.
> From Athens, Troy, Argos, Thebes, and Mycenae,
> Are taken the arguments that are suitable for these scenes.]

*Cabrières* does not completely fit the traditional patterns underlined here. If the end of the play, on par with traditional tragedies, is resolved in deaths and destruction, its temporal setting sets it apart. Indeed, if we accept that *Cabrières* was written between 1559 and 1574,[16] it seems to be one of the only plays of that time frame that deals with contemporary events (the massacre happened in 1545, the trial in 1551). I have researched historical, pre-1575 tragedies in various sources. The only other play I found based on contemporary events was François de Chantelouve's *Tragédie de feu Gaspard de Coligny* (1575), which retells the assassination of Gaspard de Colligny and of the Saint Bartholomew's Day massacre from the point of view of Catholics. Other plays that narrate previous historical events include the anonymous *Tragédie française du bon Kanut, roi de Danemark*, also from 1575, which narrates the story of King Knut, who converted to Christianity in the early eleventh century, and the *Tragédie française*

---

[14] Leblanc, *Les Écrits théoriques*, 304.

[15] Pierre de Ronsard, *Œuvres complètes*, ed. Gustave Cohen (Paris: Pléiade, 1950), 2:923.

[16] See note 1 in the translation.

*Analyzing Cabrières* 25

*à huit personnages* by Jean Bretog (1570), based on events that Bretog argued he witnessed himself in Paris and that were, according to him, known in the city where he lived around 1566–67.[17] Likewise, and because of its historical background, there are no gods, kings, or princes in it. *Cabrières* violently exposed the massacre of the Waldensians, in a Senecan manner, so that all would remember it.[18]

### Violence as a Means of Historicization

The tragedy narrates the last stand of the village of Cabrières. When the play starts, the Waldensians have repelled yet another attack by the French forces. Poulin and Catderousse, two French officials, criticize d'Opède, their leader, and blame him for their failure. D'Opède, in a long monologue, decides to dispel the doubts he has about the legitimacy of their mission and chooses to follow the violent behavior of his men. The Chorus, a ragtag group of prisoners from the villages that have previously been destroyed by the Catholics, foresees the end of the village (1v–4v). In order to breach the defenses of Cabrières, d'Opède sends Poulin to barter with the Waldensians. This is a trap, as d'Opède plans to not respect the truce, and on the contrary intends to use the occasion to invade the village and kill the villagers. Poulin discusses with the Mayor and the Syndic, the two representatives of the village. While they have opposing ideas on the matter, they eventually accept the offer. They also agree to write the main points of their faith, as d'Opède demanded, and deliver it to Poulin (5r–25v). Poulin is changed by the experience and, converted, tells d'Opède he will not help him destroy the village. D'Opède deceitfully asks him to have the Waldensians let his troops leave through the village. However, he uses this opportunity to massacre the villagers. Poulin, horrified that his actions led to the death of those he considered his brothers, commits suicide. The French troops, led by Catderousse, destroy the village and kill everybody. The Mayor, the Syndic, and the Chorus are led to the pyre, but are hopeful that their deaths will inspire their fellow Waldensians to never give up on their beliefs (26r–35v).

Because its source material is a historic massacre, violence is central to the play; it builds the relation between the different characters and finds its climax in the narration of the destruction of the city. Present throughout the tragedy, it culminates in the six pages narrating the destruction of the village (32ar–32av, 32r–33v) and all the horrible events that occurred at that time. The description of the destruction of Cabrières is extremely graphic and does not shy away from gruesome details. The events are dramatically narrated and focus on the horror

---

[17] See notably the introduction to the play by Régine Reynolds-Cornell in Enea Balmas and Michel Dassonville, eds., *La Tragédie à l'époque d'Henri II et de Charles IX. Première Série*, vol. 4, *1568–1573* (Florence: Olschki, 1999), 133–76.

[18] Louise Frappier notes the resemblance in "La Topique de la fureur dans la tragédie française du XVIe siècle." *Études françaises* 36, no. 1 (2000): 29–47, doi:10.7202/036169ar.

committed by the Catholics. In the six pages describing the massacre, I found forty-seven terms referring to death, violence, blood, and horror. Poulin contextualizes the massacre through the actions of d'Opède:

> "Soldiers," he said, "soldiers, we have just begun!
> Do not think, no, no! That it is time for us to stop.
> Kill, kill, kill! For their belongings
> I will not receive, if one of them escapes.
> Do you wish to spare the enemies of the pope?
> Kill, soldiers, kill!" And, while he was shouting, he
> Watched his murderers. His heart was benumbed,
> And he shouted more loudly at them to disregard, in their killings,
> Age or sex, sobbing or tears. (32ar–32av)

The act of killing is dissociated from the mission that was imposed upon them. Killing here is associated with the idea of personal gain, and devoid of pity. The killings are no longer motivated by the necessity to enforce the law, but rather with quasi-animalistic emotions—lust, anger—thus underlining how these acts are committed in bad faith and, by definition, are unfair and criminal.

Two events (the summary execution outside of the city and the burning of women and children in the church) are represented in the strongest emotional terms to condemn their perpetrators. D'Opède is a "torturer"; his actions against the Waldensians show that he became judge and executioner. He wants his victims to suffer as much as possible, as Poulin notes: "Because a quick death, without suffering, would not please them!" (33r). Pleasure is associated with suffering; the primary objective, which is to have a royal edict obeyed, becomes secondary and comes after the desire for cruelty that they exert. This mechanism is, of course, part of the writing device used by the author to emphasize the horror perpetuated by the royal troops, but also an amplifier of their actions. Poulin describes the atrocious view of mothers being thrown, half dead already because they were pierced by weapons, in the fire, where they burn with their children, still in their arms:

> Their mouths and their arms, in the blaze,
> Still embraced their little ones that they saw turn
> Into big pieces of ember; and finally, alongside their children,
> They not so much saw, but felt their bodies consumed by flames. (33r)

The Chorus discusses these horrors, explaining that these women would not have suffered if they did not have children:

> Poor women! Why did you become mothers?
> Had you never conceived, your deaths would be lighter,
> For you would not have witnessed, in the fire,

Your children and nephews, who were cruelly put to burn with you!
Neither you nor your children would have died together. (33r)

The Chorus and Poulin condemn the actions of the Catholics, with undisputable evidence and testimonies. The audience is a witness of these two events: the killing of so many innocents, as it is represented by the play, becomes the evidence of their martyrdom, for all to see; the audience becomes witnesses and can give testimony of what happened.[19] Andrea Frisch explains that someone becomes a witness—"and thus eligible to give testimonial evidence—the moment he gains knowledge of an event or circumstance through firsthand experience."[20] Hence, the massacre, as horrible as it was, is justified by its importance for the future of the movement. Because their names will not be forgotten, they will flourish, fulfilling the last will of the Chorus.[21] They will remain victorious through death, claiming their place in heaven. The massacre itself is the main protagonist of *Cabrières*, and the behavior of the different characters unfurls around its development. If, as Leblanc explains, putting a distance between events and their representation allowed for an experience of traumatic events from the past that was relatively pain-free, *Cabrières*, on the contrary, considers that event and representation should be as close to each other as possible. Thus, it does not shy away from exposing gaping wounds that still hurt; the pain of the massacre has to be relived, in order to prevent its memories from disappearing. The audience had to be confronted with these horrors, so that they remained vivid, to prove that such atrocities happened in the near past. These horrors are exposed to prevent them from disappearing from the discourse on religion and the wars. Since the play was likely written shortly after the trial found the principal culprit not guilty, it is, in a sense, the real and only condemnation of d'Opède and his men, who are symbolically sentenced by the anonymous writer of the play.

### Communities and Their Emotional Components

Two opposite communities are facing each other in the play: the Catholic armies and the villagers. The Catholics are composed of three members, Poulin, Catderousse, and d'Opède. The play starts with a clear opposition between Poulin

---

[19] For an analysis of witness and testimony in the Renaissance, see Andrea Frisch, *The Invention of the Eyewitness: Witnessing and Testimony in Early Modern France* (Chapel Hill: University of North Carolina Press, 2004).

[20] Frisch, *Invention of the Eyewitness*, 21.

[21] May for one Cabrières and one Mérindol
A thousand churches be born and flourish in France,
Which will drive away with your truth
The ignorance of the French, seduced too much by the Roman Antichrist. (35r)

and Catderousse, who are soldiers,[22] and d'Opède, their leader,[23] for whom they do not have any respect. If the mockeries of Catderousse and Poulin originally only target d'Opède's lack of military skills, they soon take a more personal turn. They blame his lack of military power on personal weaknesses; he is fearful ("He whose heart is frozen by fear knows not how to act"), ignorant ("How good is it not to know anything!"), and, generally, inept:

> Whoever sees himself as the leader of a powerful army,
> If valor is deeply engraved in his heart,
> Would never let the enemy grow strong. (2r)

They completely destroy not only his authority but also his status as a warring man, when they sarcastically claim: "What a leader! What a governor! What a bold warrior!" (2v). He is in a sense demasculinized because they consider that his actions are in complete opposition with their definitions of what a leader should be.

These attacks severely impact d'Opède; he is full of doubts on his mission. He is also highly doubtful that his orders are legitimate:

> Is it determined, then, that you will never
> Leave me alone an hour, oh you wretched conscience?
> Why do I want all of these people to be massacred?
> This faithful people, wholly devoted to God!
> This people, whose life is so blessedly pure,
> That for their love God still tolerates us? (3v–4r)

What we have here is an opposition in the thought of d'Opède between his duties as a leader and his opinion and morality. He wonders if his mentality as a man has to be in harmony with his duties as a leader. His doubts and questions bring together the opposition that is at the core of his personality. The construction of his masculinity is torn between the demands of his role as a leader and his duty to achieve his objectives, but also his emotional questioning as a human being who

---

[22] The Vianney edition is the only one to provide the reader with a list of characters preceding the play. Catderousse is described as the "lieutenant des armées du roi" (lieutenant of the armies of the king), while Poulin is "capitaine des armées du roi, baron de la garde" (captain of the armies of the king, lord of the guards): Joseph Vianney, ed., *La Tragédie du sac de Cabrières, tragédie inédite en vers français du XVIe siècle. Publiée avec une introduction historique par Fernand Benoit et une etude littéraire de J. Vianey* (Marseille: Institut historique de Provence, 1927), 27.

[23] Gabriel Audisio explains, "Jean Maynier, baron of Opède, was responsible both for justice, as the president of the Parlement in Aix, and the police, as the absent governor's lieutenant"; see *The Waldensian Dissent: Persecution and Survival, c. 1170–c. 1570*, trans. Claire Davidson (Cambridge: Cambridge University Press, 1999), 191.

witnesses what he believes to be unfairness against a people that he himself recognizes to be protected by God. It is in a long monologue that d'Opède changes his personality.[24] He is literally torn between his sympathy for the Waldensians, and what they represent, and his duties as the leader of a force that has to fight these ideals. He expresses sympathy and even some kind of admiration for the Waldensians. Their piety is great: "God is taking their cause in hand"; they have never plotted against France: "Prayers always granted for the king" (4r). D'Opède himself realizes that he is facing an insolvable problem; if they are innocent and pious, why should they be punished? This moment is pivotal, because it is then that d'Opède realizes that he has qualities that he chooses to put forward to construct himself as a strong leader.

Even though his reflection leads him to reconsider the foundations of his military persona, it is nevertheless his actions as a military leader that trigger his introspection:

> Have I *struck down* Cabrierette, have I *ruined* Mérindol,
> *Sacked* Saint Martin, have I *ransacked*
> Twenty villages, towns, or castles, have I *turned them to ashes*,
> As if they were never anything but *furnaces*,
> Have I then *destroyed* so many men and places
> To be pitiful instead of furious,
> So that, by sparing this *despicable rabble*,
> I yield to them the fruit of my battles? (4v)

The emphasis on the vocabulary related to destruction is these lines is my own. Whereas the first part of d'Opède's speech is full of doubts and questions, it becomes here extremely proactive. His doubts are washed away by the reality of his past achievements. His emotional focus starts shifting, with the opposition between pity and fury, between his before and his now, which is also destined to become his future. He turns into a bloodthirsty creature, whose emotions are geared toward the destruction of the Waldensians: "They will all die, from the first to the last ranks, / Or today I will cover Cabrières all in blood" (4v). He symbolically destroys his former self and negates his personality by turning his attention toward new, different emotions. It does not mean, however, that he becomes an emotionless executor. His emotional behavior now condones anger, fear, and aggression as a new model for his persona. By accepting to become the leader that his men want to have, he does not erase himself but, on the contrary, transforms his persona into a suitable one to fit in with his men; his conversion to violence is complete.

---

[24] It covers three pages, from 3v to 4v.

## Poulin as d'Opède's Foil?

While d'Opède voluntarily changes his personality, Poulin's transformation is a revelation. At the beginning of his mission, he is aware of the risks; in spite of the lack of stage direction, a few of his reactions in the play are said aside, as a reflection of his inner feelings.[25] He is facing the two leaders of Cabrières, two men with drastically different views on his proposal. They are simply named for their functions as mayor and syndic.[26] The Mayor is the most critical of the two concerning the demands of Poulin. He understands that Poulin will betray them. From the very beginning, he shows his distrust. More than being reserved, he is angry at Poulin; he is also distraught that his fellow leader is letting such treachery deceive him:

> Can you not feel the poison of d'Opède!
> Or, if you do, are you not trying to remedy it?
> Alas! Do you not recognize this deceitful Poulin?
> This deceitful Poulin, swollen with a duplicitous and malevolent spirit,
> This deceitful Poulin, who was nurtured by the Turks,
> This deceitful Poulin, who makes all virtues vices,
> This deceitful Poulin, who believes in God like a horse,
> This villain (do believe me!) forges our ruin,
> And he is coming to slit our throats with our own knives! (9r)

The two key emotional traits of the Mayor are anger and hatred. He explains all the evil brought by Poulin, because of his education and his status, and how they are opposed to his supposed call to peace. Only death can result from trusting him. His anger is not only directed toward the Catholics but also toward his fellow Waldensians, who cannot accept that there is anything real or good coming from this demand. The impact of his anger is of particular importance because it is done on a public stage (in front of two other protagonists), whereas d'Opède's emotional change was largely done in private.

Whereas the Mayor is extremely critical and doubtful, the Syndic behaves entirely differently toward Poulin, as he encourages a possible peaceful resolution to the siege: "We must, by any means, but not by force, / Push the enemy to admit his error" (9v). Whereas the Mayor is very pragmatic and sees how Poulin is the sign of the destruction of Cabrières, the Syndic puts his trust in God first and foremost and wants to believe that violence is not the solution to their cur-

---

[25] Before the conversation with the two Waldensians starts, he addresses his fears: "These captives have followed me. They take counsel with each other / And, trembling, I can hear them speaking from here" (8v). After the Mayor discusses the fact that Poulin is probably coming to destroy them, Poulin is horrified and terribly scared: "I am finished, I am discovered, I am dead!" (9r). He also realizes that he has to be careful if he does not want to be caught: "I have to undermine this cunning man" (11v).

[26] A syndic was a municipal magistrate in Provence.

*Analyzing Cabrières* 31

rent problems. Both present two potential resolutions to the same problem, one with positive consequences, the other with a disastrous outcome. In the end, it is the decision to trust Poulin that matters. The Syndic is a genuinely trusting man, who wants to see in every element the mark of God:

> We are grateful to God, for he granted his grace
> To you, who were deceived before
> By the guile of Satan, and he showed you his way,
> In which he keeps whoever follows it from being led astray.
> We are grateful to him for your decision
> To free us, and bring happiness upon us,
> At least if this happens as you just explained. (13r)

God is the reason not only for their presence on Earth, but also for all the events that already happened and that will happen to them. During the whole play, predestination is mainly present in the words of the Syndic. As these lines show, all these events happened because God willed them. Because he is present in every single event of the life of the Waldensians, even the harshest ones, everything must be accepted, as they are the direct consequence of his will. One of the tricks of d'Opède is to ask for the profession of faith of Cabrières that he will bring to the king.[27] Because he trusts Poulin, the Syndic agrees with his demands. When he gives their profession of faith to Poulin ("We acknowledge all these points. Here for our part are / The articles of our faith written one by one, / Sealed and marked," 14r), he also gives a divine acknowledgment that what is happening is a sign of the presence of God. Even though this justifies Poulin's lies, it also demonstrates how much their love of God is superior even to their will to live. Poulin's treachery, directly leading to the martyrdom of Cabrières, is classic in Protestant literature.[28] It reinforces the anti-Catholic dimension of the play: the Catholics are portrayed, via Poulin, as people who use the piety of the Waldensians, and their love of God, as tools to destroy them. But even with the apparent opposition between the Mayor and the Syndic, they are both professing, in different ways, profound love for God, their religion, and their city.

The Mayor and the Syndic are two very different men. However, their shared emotional connection to Cabrières is the same. Both exemplify how different emotional approaches can be linked to the same postulate, namely the defense

---

[27] So that Poulin might better complete his work,
And so that none of them discover who he truly is,
I will detain them in speaking of their faith.
Friends, we have no need to go to the king.
If you expose the principles of your religion to me here,
I will listen without saying a thing. (17v)

[28] See Franck Lestringant, *Lumière des martyrs: Essai sur le martyre au siècle des réformes* (Paris: Honoré Champion, 2004).

and well-being of their city. However, they appear to be drastically uneven and nonmoderated in their emotional approach to Poulin. If the definition of a good leader is to allow his people to be safe and to stand strong when faced with adversity,[29] the judicious leader should not, however, accept to do any foul action to reach his goal. The ideas of the Mayor and of the Syndic are both highly emotional but focus on different elements (anger and hatred of the enemy vs. love of peace and respect for negotiations); since they are the bicephalous figure of governance in Cabrières, their joint actions demonstrate strong leadership, and their intentions cannot be discussed, as their only interest is to safeguard their people.

Poulin is impressed by these two men and becomes a sponge that absorbs their emotions and relation to God. He has an epiphany and converts to their cause. His conversion, however, is not textually presented. He never clearly expresses his change of religion. Evidence of this can be seen in his new stance toward the inhabitants of Cabrières: "I will not slay you, nor will I be their killer" (26v). D'Opède is much more direct in the revelation of the change in Poulin and directly addresses the "conversion" to the audience: "But who is this fellow, who is coming straight toward me? / Is this Poulin? Yes, it is whom I see" (21v). This evolution of Poulin between two groups is decisive in the development of the play, since both entities are interconnected by the movement of their members.

The two groups (the Catholic armies and the Waldensians) are not immovably distinct; this could be seen as an "interaffective fluidity," which allows for the deconstruction and reconstruction of emotional interactions within the two groups and between them. This fluidity, inherent to the evolution of emotional feelings, explains how some members of an already united family may feel the urge to readjust themselves (as was the case for d'Opède) or, on the contrary, may feel attracted to another set of emotional rules. The (re)creation of the self through emotional narratives[30]—in the case of *Cabrières*, through a reassessment of the equilibrium between needs and beliefs—enables the fluid transposition of one member from one group to the other, or even its evolution within a group. If d'Opède has always been a member of the community of the army, it is only through a reassessment of his emotions that he was finally able to be accepted by his men. Concerning Poulin, it is through conversion—even if it is

---

[29] Erasmus explains in *Education of a Christian Prince*, "it is the prince's duty to keep everything peaceful and harmonious"; ed. Neil M. Cheshire and Michael J. Heath (Cambridge: Cambridge University Press, 1997), 59. Jean Bodin, one of the chief French thinkers on the power, duties, and rules governing a prince or a leader, argues in his *Les Six livres de la république* (1576) that "waging war or negotiating for peace . . . is one of the most important points of greatness"; ed. Gerard Mairet (Paris: Le Livre de poche, 1993), 101 (décerner la guerre ou traiter la paix . . . est l'un des plus grands points de la majesté).

[30] See Robyn Fivush, "Defining and Regulating the Self through Emotion Narratives," in *Changing Emotions*, ed. D. Hermans et al. (New York: Psychology Press, 2013), 10–16.

# Analyzing Cabrières

not recognized and accepted by the Waldensians—that he channeled his emotional change that made him renounce his mission of destruction, to embrace his newly found love for the piety of Cabrières.

### Religion, between Pretext and Context

The emotional creation and disruption of the two communities aforementioned is first and foremost motivated by the weight and power of God in their lives. It is because the Waldensians wanted to abide by their religious beliefs that they were hunted down and massacred. It is because of this massacre that they became martyrs and are celebrated as such in histories and collections on martyrology. Finally, it is because of their religiosity that their stories were theatricalized in tragedy.[31] In *Cabrières*, religion sets up the development of the two communities, depending on their reaction to not only the worship, but also how it is organized, and the place of God in their everyday lives.

As surprising as it may be, *Cabrières* is not a play that proposes an opposition between a "good religion" and a "bad religion." Whereas God and faith are central to the Waldensians, for the Catholics, they do not seem to be a significant issue. Contrary to traditional Protestant attacks on Catholic dogma in Renaissance reformist fiction,[32] there are very few direct attacks on the faith of the royal armies and almost no references to religion or God in the words of either Catderousse, Poulin, or d'Opède (before their transformation). Instead, there is what I would define as an abandonment of God by the Catholics, particularly with Catderousse, whose behavior seems almost irreligious.

Olivier Millet describes Catderousse as a beast with no qualm or conscience,[33] as his motivations seem very materialistic:

---

[31] Basing his analysis on David El Kenz's *Les Bûchers du roi: La culture protestante des martyrs (1523–1572)* (Seyssel: Champ Valon, 1997), Jameson Tucker identifies in "From Fire to Iron: Martyrs and Massacre Victims in Genevan Martyrology," in *Dying, Death, Burial and Commemoration in Reformation Europe*, edited by Elizabeth C. Tingle and Jonathan Willis (Farnham: Ashgate, 2015), 161–62, five signs that must be present in order to identify a person or a community as martyrs, according to Crespin:
1) Martyrs must shed blood;
2) The doctrine at issue, and not punishment, qualifies the martyr;
3) A judgment must have sentenced their choice of faith over life;
4) They must have been condemned for a spiritual reason;
5) The martyr must be constant, and not have recanted or rescinded his faith to the authorities.

[32] See Luc Racault, *Hatred in Print: Catholic Propaganda and Protestant Identity during the French Wars of Religion* (London: Ashgate, 2002). Racault notably reveals that most attacks against the Catholics at the time focused on their false interpretation of the scriptures and their subjection to Rome, considered to be demeaning.

[33] Millet, "Vérité et mensonge," 268.

As I am certain we will be victorious,
I set our soldiers ablaze with the fire of glory:
"Soldiers! If your hearts are as strong as they once were,
They will be beaten for sure! So, forward! Spur your horses onward!
The first of you who sets foot on their walls
Will earn, besides honor, this richly adorned medal,
And he who comes next, my chain made of pure gold!
The third and the fourth will also earn great prizes. (5r–5v)

Catderousse buys the courage of his men and does not praise the grandeur of their actions or the greatness that they will bring to the kingdom. He harnesses the power of greed to have the soldiers follow him. He even mocks the Waldensians and their appeal to God: "The cowards already pray God, as if they surrender already" (5v).

While Catderousse could be accused of ignoring God, Poulin and d'Opède use him in their scheme. In the course of his attempt to accomplish a truce with Cabrières, Poulin uses God's name in order to trick the Waldensians:

O sovereign Lord, who holds everything in your hand!
Lord, who forbids us from taking your name in vain,
And who condemned for perjury
Those who scornfully swore in your name for nothing!
O Lord, who destroys the traitors and liars
And who sees deep in the abyss of our hearts
I beg you, Eternal Father, to unleash on me
Your lightning and your thunderbolts, your exploding thunderstorm.
May they now burn me, excluded from salvation,
If, for this holy people, trapped in this encampment,
I have not taken arms and found a way
Today to save and deliver Cabrières. (13v)

In complete opposition to the armies, the Waldensians are not only pious, but also live for and through God. While the Catholics use religion as a pretext, for the Waldensians, everything is put into the context of religion, making it the most important part of their lives, around which they organize their entire life. When Poulin comes to propose the truth, they wonder whether Catderousse could "Also hear and love the Gospels?" (10r). Their beliefs are expressed at length in the profession of faith that is required by d'Opède to leave. This very long excerpt (17v–21v, ten pages in the manuscript) is the core of religiosity of the play. Even though it is a declaration following a demand by d'Opède, the Mayor and the Syndic present a life guide for whoever wants to follow in their footsteps. They present their faith through an interwoven dialogue between the two dignitaries, who complete each other's ideas, echo, respond, and discuss their faith.

The profession of faith is developed around a progressive model. First, God is the creator of the world and everything; he can destroy and punish as quickly

*Analyzing Cabrières* 35

as he created, but also rewards and embellishes (17v–18v). God created man, and gave him all the gifts possible; yet, humankind does not follow the footsteps of God and betrays his trust through sin (18v–20r). The only possible redemption will come through death, which is the only and genuine way to eternal life, to follow the footsteps of Christ (20r–20v). Finally, it is only complete and unconditional love of God that brings redemption and eternal life (20v–21v). The immortality of God makes him the only savior; it also puts the Waldensian faith in context. There are never any references to the clergy; only obedience and worship of God can save his people. He is the first and foremost basis of their faith, "distinct in three persons" (17v). As the creator of life, he is the sole entity worthy of being worshiped. The long profession of faith is, of course, the presentation of the beliefs of the Waldensians, but also of their conception of the world. It is their pride, their life, but, unfortunately, also the confirmation of their demise. When d'Opède has heard it, he already knows that they will be destroyed:

> Enough! I am leaving, since I do not believe you,
> Just as you do not believe in the pope, priests, or clergymen.
> Enough! I do not want to continue this conversation.
> It is time for me to join my people and follow them. (29r)

The condemnation of d'Opède is very harsh and definitive. As he is presented as a nonbeliever, these words of pure dedication to God are impossible to bear. His desire to put an end to their speech seems to be another example of the pure nature of their actions. They are speaking the words of God through their actions, and their faith that they have presented is God's world uttered in words. D'Opède, as Millet reminds us,[34] is by definition deceitful and untrustworthy; he is then hurt by the justice of God, present in the speech of the Waldensians. By joining his people, the destruction of the city is ineluctable, which the Chorus foreshadows.

### The Chorus, an Emotional Space

The Chorus is widely present throughout the text, spanning thirty-eight pages out of the seventy-two in the manuscript. Notably, it speaks in four very long expository monologues. The first one (6r–8v) is a reflection on the nature of victory, and on how God grants it — or not. The second one (14v–17r) centers on the disastrous effects that foul, deceitful speech can have on people's minds; examples from the Bible are used in demonstration (Sodom, the Golden calf, Samaria). Its third monologue, also the longest (22r–25v), balances the previous declaration on the power of words by underlining how God's discourse is powerful, beautiful, and filled with love. Finally, its last long declaration (29v–32r) follows the treason of Poulin and the beginning of the martyrdom of Cabrières.

---

[34] See Millet, "Vérité et mensonge," 268.

The Chorus explains how death and destruction are a path to God, and how those who remain close to God will find respite in his kingdom, whereas the others will be punished, foreshadowing the execution of the Chorus on the pyre.

The Chorus is a symbolic personification of Fate. It represents the past, the present, and the future of the Waldensians. It also represents an inextricable trajectory toward death and destruction, counterbalanced by the promise of martyrdom. In its first lines, the Chorus introduces itself as a group of survivors of Mérindol: "From the cruel and deadly sack of Mérindol, / A captive troop we remain in the camp of these brigands" (3r). Its members are Waldensians who have witnessed the horrors endured by their people under the yoke of d'Opède and his men. The Chorus serves as a symbol of the victims of their horror; it is also the messenger of death, presenting and foretelling the demise of Cabrières. In fact, this collective entity that speaks as one person is already dying: "As for us, our lives must be taken by slow fire" (3r). This allusion to the fire foreshadows its fate when they will be forced into the pyre and will be burned. It represents a faith that cannot be defeated, through which the elements of the play are unfolding. The role of the Chorus in theater is crucial, yet it can be hard to decipher. In Greek tragedies, the Chorus was a central entity in the play, due to its enduring presence on stage, as well as through its condition as a messenger between action, location, and audience, acting as an omniscient entity in the play.[35] In Cabrières, the Chorus has a liminal role in the action itself, both in the unfolding of the elements and also in the development of temporal tropes and localized representations of the massacre.

The Chorus was traditionally seen as the representation of the vision of the author. In his Dictionnaire du théâtre, Fabrice Pavis explains it as "consisting of agent(s), nonindividualized and frequently abstract, representing moral and higher political interests."[36] In Cabrières, the Chorus is not abstract. On the contrary, it is an explicit representation of the Waldensians who have already been subdued, foreshadowing the fate of Cabrières. What it declares is based on its experience and is geared toward its fellow Waldensians, but also toward the audience. There is no scenic indication about the action, the location, or the actors. As the members of the Chorus were brought with the armies, their presence onstage is a visual explanation of the violence of war, which also constructs the space of history in the space of theater. The Chorus is Mérindol; however, throughout the play, it evolves toward a much more universal presence. The experience of the massacre is inscribed in its persona, because it was a victim and still suffers

---

[35] See David Wiles, Tragedy in Athens: Performance Stage and Theatrical Meaning (Cambridge: Cambridge University Press, 1997), particularly chaps. 4 ("The Mimetic Action of the Chorus") and 5 ("The Chorus: Its Transformation of Stage")

[36] Fabrice Pavis, Dictionnaire du théâtre (Paris: Dunod, 1996), 44: "composé de forces(s) non individualisées et souvent abstraites, représentant des intérêts moraux ou politiques supérieurs."

the consequences. Nothing can be done to prevent such a massacre from happening again because it is literally entrapped, which reinforces its incapacity to help their Waldensian brothers. The Chorus is the entire space of sacrifice of the play, embodying the principles of the faith: pious belief and total submission to God, denunciation of deceitful language, and acceptance of its fate.

## Conclusion

*Cabrières* provided its audience with an emotional performance of history, in which its theatricalization is shaped into an act of resistance and testimony against horror. The twenty years (approximately) between the actual massacre and its representation cover much of the first skirmishes and full-out battles that tore apart the French kingdom; in a period when Protestants were exterminated because of their faith, the play offers not only a condemnation of these actions but also evidence of the premeditation of such a massacre. The wars of religion were a battle of propaganda and counterpropaganda, in which both camps were trying to undermine each other through injurious attacks and slander. Not only were Protestants destroyed physically, but their legacy and memory had to be wiped out as well, through narratives produced by royal forces. Lies were produced, the truth was manipulated, in order to create a discourse that reinforced the power of the king against the heretics. David LaGuardia explains, "those in power had to manipulate constantly what was said, where it was said, how it was interpreted, how it was communicated in a textual form . . . and the ways in which it was remembered."[37] *Cabrières* is a testimony of resistance, proving the horrors and lies of the kingdom, and asserting the truth of Waldensianism and, by association, of the Reformed churches in general. *Cabrières* makes sure that the deaths of the Waldensians will not be forgotten. Through the play—and its inerasable presence on paper—they keep their place in religious history (how and why they became martyrs), in legal history, and also in the general history of France. The emotionality of the play, finally, inscribes it in the emotional history of the wars, thus permitting these testimonies to endure.

---

[37] David P. LaGuardia, "Two Queens, a Dog, and a Purloined Letter: On Memory as a Discursive Phenomenon in Late Renaissance France," in *Memory and Community in Sixteenth-Century France*, ed. David P. LaGuardia and Cathy Yandell (Farnham: Ashgate, 2015), 36.

# EDITING THE MANUSCRIPT

When a scholar starts working on a critical edition and/or a translation of a text from the Middle Ages or the Renaissance, selecting which manuscript or manuscripts to use is crucial. For instance, the *Roman de Renart*, one of the most famous texts of the French Middle Ages, exists in twenty-seven different manuscripts.[1] The *Tragedy of the Sack of Cabrières* differs from most other works in that there is only one manuscript of the play, Pal. lat. 1983, at the Biblioteca Apostolica Vaticana, in the Palatine Fond. All the previous modern editions of the play are based on Pal. lat. 1983; thanks to the digitization made by the Üniversitätsbibliothek Heidelberg, it is available online for free.[2] It is composed of thirty-six folios sewn together, forming an octavo volume. The pages themselves are paper, bound in white leather, which Karl Christ identifies as pigskin.[3] The text is not printed, but handwritten. The writing is very clear; the pages are numbered and void of any cross-outs. Folio 1v even has an illuminated letter at the beginning of the first word of the text, the *U* of "un."[4] This is, however, the only illumination of the text, with a fleur-de-lis drawn underneath the title on folio 1v. The text is not divided into acts or scenes; instead, a list of characters is presented before what would be the different acts; there is no demarcation for scenes. One of the yet unanswerable questions about *Cabrières* is why no other manuscript of the play has been found. This might have always been intended to be the only version of the play. It might have been performed, and the Duke of Bavaria, the dedicatee of the play,[5] may have witnessed it and liked it, and hence was gifted a copy of it, written for the occasion. It might also have never

---

[1] The Archives de Littérature du Moyen-âge is a good, regularly updated source for the location of manuscripts: https://www.arlima.net/qt/renart_roman_de.html.

[2] Available online: http://digi.ub.uni-heidelberg.de/diglit/bav_pal_lat_1983/.

[3] See Karl Christ, ed., *Tragédie du sac de Cabrières: Ein Kalvinistisches Drama der Reformationszeit* (Halle: Max Niemeyer, 1928). Christ explains that in order to protect the book from the duress of transportation ("um die Schwierigkeiten des Transportes zu mindern") the book was bound in pigskin ("mit einem glatten Schweinsledereinband versehen worden," 28).

[4] The numeration I chose to follow in this book is that of the digitized copy at Heidelberg. That is why folios are numbered starting with the first written page, and not the first page of the actual manuscript.

[5] See the dedication on fol. 1r.

been published because it did not have any success. Another question about the play is how, if, and when it was performed. I have not located any contemporary document that allowed me to find any information on this subject. Karl Christ does not mention anything; in the Benoit/Vianey edition there are allusions as to what the stage could have looked like, but there is no evidence in the critical apparatus of whether and when it was performed.[6] It is impossible to know the whereabouts of the performance of the play in the sixteenth century, and unless new manuscripts and documents on the play are unearthed, these questions and hypotheses are likely to remain unanswered.

## Modern Editions of the Play

There are only three modern editions of the text. The edition I propose here is the fourth, and the first translation into English. Joseph Vianey and Fernand Benoit edited and published the play for the first time in 1927. In 1928, Karl Christ published another edition, with a critical apparatus in German.[7] It is interesting that such an obscure play (at the time) was edited and published twice in a period when it was barely known. Even though the Vianey/Benoit edition was published first, Christ explains in his introduction that his work is based on his own discovery of the text in 1913.[8] The 1927 edition does not make any reference to the original manuscript. Finally, it was not until 1990 that the play was published again, edited by Daniela Boccassini, and included in *La Tragédie à l'époque d'Henri II et de Charles IX. Première Série.*[9] The chart below summarizes the content of the three editions.

---

[6] See *La Tragédie du sac de Cabrières, tragédie inedite en vers français du XVIe siècle. Publiée avec une introduction historique par Fernand Benoit et une etude littéraire de J. Vianey* (Marseille: Institut historique de Provence, 1927): "L'action de la pièce se passe toute entière au camp catholique. Mais on peut supposer que le décor pouvant, suivant les habitudes du temps, representer plusieurs lieux, représente plusieurs partie du camp: la tente de d'Opède, l'endroit où le choeur est tenu prisonnier, etc." (viii) (the action of the whole play takes place in the encampment of the Catholic troops. However one can imagine that the scenery could represent various parts of the encampment, based on the customs of the time: d'Opède's tent, the place where the Chorus is held captive, etc.).

[7] See notes 3 and 6.

[8] "Das Drama ist in einer einzigen Handschrifft erhalten, dem Codex Pal. Lat 1983 der Vaticana, den ich im Jahre 1913 unter des noch unbekannten französischen Handschriften der alten Heidelberger Bibliotheken gefunden und an anderer Stelle bereits kurz beschrieben habe" (Christ, *Tragédie du sac de Cabrières*, 26) (This play is the only handwritten piece in Codex Pal. lat. 1983 of the Vatican Library, which I found in 1913, in the still unknown French manuscript of the old Library at Heidelberg, on which I have written elsewhere).

[9] Daniela Boccassini, ed., *La Tragédie du sac de Cabrières*, in *La Tragédie à l'époque d'Henri II et de Charles IX. Première Série*, vol. 3, *1566–1567*, ed. Régine Reynolds Cornell

# Editing the Manuscript

| Fernand Benoit /<br>Joseph Vianey (1927) | Karl Christ (1928) | Daniela Boccassini (1990) |
|---|---|---|
| *Preface*:<br><br>pp. v–viii: Historical origins of the genre in the Renaissance<br><br>pp. viii–xvii: Summary of the play with cultural and literary references<br><br>pp. xvii–xviii: Qualities of the play<br><br>*Critical apparatus*:<br><br>pp. 1–4: History of the massacre, with literary references to other massacres in the sixteenth century<br><br>pp. 4–9: History of the Waldensians<br><br>pp. 9–25: The march to the massacre, its unfolding, and its consequences<br><br>pp. 27–28: List of characters, summary of the play | pp. 1–6: History of the massacre<br><br>pp. 6–13: Contemporary retelling of the Luberon massacres<br><br>pp. 14–22: Changes and similarities between the event and its retelling in the play<br><br>pp. 23–26: The religiosity of the play<br><br>pp. 26–28: Analysis of the manuscript<br><br>pp. 28–36: Analysis of the dedicatee, and its importance in the dating of the manuscript<br><br>pp. 36–48: Literary relevance of the play and analysis<br><br>pp. 48–58: Summary of the play, rhetorical and rhythmical elements<br><br>pp. 127–28: Excerpt from the *Histoire des martyrs* | pp. 205–9: History of the massacre<br><br>pp. 209–14: Literary references and summary of the play<br><br>pp. 214–18: Analysis of the themes<br><br>pp. 219–20: Bibliography |

**Table 1:** Contents of the critical apparatus of the three modern editions of the play.

The different editions all stress the importance of the historical context of the destruction of the Waldensian communities in Provence in order to understand the play. The same elements are generally present in each analysis, with references to the Judgment of Mérindol, to the works of Jean Crespin and Jacques Aubéry for the proceedings of the actions leading to the massacre, to the destruction itself, and to its aftermath. Christ presents excerpts from Crespin, which are completely absent from any other edition. Boccassini uses the correspondence

---

et al., Théâtre français de la Renaissance 3 (Paris: Presses Universitaires de France; Florence: L. S. Olschki, 1990), 203–78.

of Pietro Gelido, treasurer of the Pontifical legation and main organizer of the military expedition, as the historical reference for her retelling of the events.[10] Benoit and Vianey base their studies on many examples coming from similar literature on martyrdom.

### Editing the Text: Words and Format

The biggest point of discordance between the three editions is the transcription of the original manuscript. Vianey and Benoit decided to divide the play into parts, while Christ and Boccassini chose to keep the original format of the play. Boccassini argues in her introduction that this model could be compared to that of Greek tragedy, which was also devoid of divisions, because of the presence of long monologues of the Chorus.[11] For *Cabrières*, the most important choice regarding the edition of the play concerns the reproduction of the text. None of the three editions have perfectly reproduced the text as is, and have chosen to make concessions and/or changes that I am going to address here. The text begins with a dialogue between Poulin, d'Opède, and Catderousse, who discuss the duties of a strong leader. Below is the original text, directly and exactly reproduced as it is present in the manuscript, on which I based my edition; I will compare it to the three other editions.[12]

**Pal. lat. 1983:**
D'Opede
Un coeur vaillant mourra plustost qu'estre vaincu
Et moy las malheureux auray ie tant vescu
Qu'à vaincre ou à mourir je prefere la fuite!

Poulin
Le Lion fuit s'il a un Cerf pour sa conduite
Ainsi le camp auquel commande un bonnet rond
Comme Neige au Soleil devant l'ennemi fond.

Catderousse
Vous vous entendez trop aux proces & enquestes
À faire fouetter à faire couper testes
Ou à faire souffrir quelque plus dure mort.

---

[10] See Boccassini, *La Tragédie du sac de Cabrières*, 205 n. 2.

[11] Boccassini, *La Tragédie du sac de Cabrières*, 215 n. 19.

[12] My choice for this edition was to reproduce the manuscript as faithfully as possible, exactly as it was handwritten by the author or scribe.

*Editing the Manuscript* 43

**Boccassini:**

In the 1990 edition, all the words have been modernized with their current forms; likewise, "Poulin" becomes "Polin." Quotation marks have been added. [13]

D'OPP Un coeur vaillant mourra **plutôt qu'être** vaincu
Et **moi**, las, malheureux, **aurai-je** tant **vécu**
Qu'à vaincre ou à mourir je **préfère** la fuite?

POLIN "Le lion fuit s'il a un cerf pour sa conduite:
Ainsi le camp auquel commande un bonnet rond
Comme neige au soleil devant l'ennemi fond.

CATD. Vous vous entendez trop aux **procès** et **enquêtes**,
A faire fouetter, à faire couper **têtes**,
Ou à faire souffrir quelque plus dure mort.

The modernization of the text eases the reading process for nonspecialists, but by doing so does not provide the reader with the original text as it was written. Boccassini, like the editors of the two other versions, also decided to add punctuation marks, following, in her case, her choice to adapt the text to modern standards.

**Christ:**

The Christ edition chose to remain relatively close to the original, but nevertheless added punctuation and changed the first-person singular pronoun. Some words were also left as they were in the manuscript:

D'Opede
Un Coeur vaillant mourra plustost qu'estre vaincu
Et moy, las malheureux! Auray je tant vescu
Que vaincre ou à mourir je prefere la fuite!

Poulin
Le Lion fuit, s'il a un cerf pour sa conduite.
Ainsi le camp auquel commande un bonnet rond
Comme **Neige** au **Soleil** devant l'ennemi fond.

Catderousse
Vous vous entendez trop aux proces et enquestes

---

[13] In the following excerpts, the editorial changes made to the original text will be put in bold script. The analysis of the different changes that were made by the previous editors of the play should not be considered as criticism of choices that were made to cope with editorial or personal demands or constraints, but rather as a comment on how these change the perception of the original manuscript, namely how this changes its physicality and its reading.

À faire fouetter, à faire couper testes,
Ou à faire souffrir quelque plus dure mort.

### Benoit/Vianey

Finally, the edition by Benoit and Vianey is very close to Christ's, with some minor changes (punctuation marks, accents) and a note explaining that the reference to d'Opède as a "bonnet rond" is made in order to mock him; lastly, the capitalization of some words was changed.

D'Opède
Un **Coeur Vaillant** mourra plustost qu'estre vaincu,
Et moy, las! Malheureux, auray-**je** tant vescu
Qu'à vaincre ou à mourir je **préfère** la fuite?

Poulin
Le lion fuit s'il a un cerf pour pour sa conduite.
Ainsi le camp, auquel commande un bonnet rond,
Comme neige au soleil devant l'ennemi fond.

Catderousse
Vous vous entendez trop aux procès **et** enquestes,
À faire fouetter, à faire couper testes,
Ou à faire souffrir quelque plus dure mort.

I reproduced the text exactly as it appears on the different folios, with signature and page numbers, and no addition of punctuation marks.

A few specificities must be noted:

- The first-person singular pronoun "je" is written throughout the manuscript either as "ie" or "je." I have kept these occurrences in my transcription of the text.

- Long *s*'s are present through the manuscript and have been converted in the edition to round *s*, so as not to be mistaken for *f*.

- Two words are presented with tildes: "canōne" (2v), "devāt" (5r). These are solely used for the nasalization of the words and have been kept as such.

All these changes are kept in the edition. I chose to translate the whole play without rhyme, in order to prioritize an exact translation of the text over stylistic imitation, and also in order to make the text easier to understand and to read.

# TRAGEDY OF THE SACK OF CABRIÈRES

[1r]                                    1

Pour tres-illustre PRINCE Monsieur
Christophle Duc de Bavieres, filz tres-aimé
De Mon Seigneur l'Electeur, & Comte
Palatin et ca.

# [1r]

To the very illustrious PRINCE, Monsieur
Christophle, Duke of Bavaria, most beloved son
Of the Lord Elector, and Count
Palatine, etc.[1]

---

[1] The "Christophle" in question must be Christof (1551–74), son of Frederick III, Elector Palatine (1515–76), as the three previous editions of the text (Vianey, Christ, and Boccassini) all agree. He died in 1574, at the Battle of Mooker Heide, during the early years of the Eighty Years' War (1568–1648), between the Seventeen Provinces (the Netherlands were mostly Protestant) and the Spanish armies of the Catholic king of Spain, Philip II. This event gives us a clearer idea of when the play was written: between 1559 (when Frederick was elected) and 1574 (when Christof died). Whereas Vianey/ Benoit extrapolate that the play might have been dedicated during Christof's sojourn in Switzerland (1566–68), Boccassini notes that this is by no means a valid method to date the play, since it could have been dedicated to him after his sojourn. For more information on Christof, see Andrew L. Thomas, *A House Divided: Wittelsbach Confessional Court Cultures in the Holy Roman Empire, c. 1550–1650* (Leiden: Brill, 2010), and Eike Wolgast, *Reformierte Konfession und Politik im 16. Jahrhundert: Studien zur Geschichte der Kurpfalz im Reformationszeitalter: vorgetragen am 9. November 1996* (Heidelberg: Universitätsverlag C. Winter, 1998).

[1v]

## TRAGEDIE
## DU SAC DE CA
## BRIERE

D'Opede Poulin & Catderousse

D'Opede
Un[1] cœur vaillant mourra plustost qu'estre vaincu
Et moy las malheureux auray ie tant vescu
Qu'à vaincre ou à mourir je prefere la fuite!

Poulin
Le Lion fuit s'il a un Cerf pour sa conduite
Ainsi le camp auquel commande un bonnet rond
Comme Neige au Soleil devant l'ennemi fond.

Catderousse
Vous vous entendez trop aux proces & enquestes
À faire fouetter à faire couper testes
Ou à faire souffrir quelque plus dure mort.

Poulin
Encor scavez vous bien du droit faire le tort
Mais comme il faut donner chaudement les alarmes
Vous vous y entendez comm'un clerc fait aux armes.

---

[1] The "u" in the manuscript is illuminated.

*Tragedy of the Sack of Cabrières* 49

[1v]

TRAGEDY
OF THE SACK OF CA
BRIÈRES

D'Opède, Poulin, and Catderousse

D'Opède
A valiant heart would rather die than be defeated.
And I, weary and wretched, have lived so long
That I prefer flight to victory or death!

Poulin
Just as the lion flees if he has a deer for a leader,
The army led by a man with a scholar's cap[1]
Melts away before its enemy, like snow in the sun.

Catderousse
You rely too much[2] on trials, inquests,
On whipping, or on beheading,
Or on making people suffer even harsher deaths.[3]

Poulin
What is more, you know how to make a wrong of a right.
But when one must valiantly go to war,
You are as expert as a clerk who bears arms.

---

[1] The original French expression, "bonnet rond," refers to the kind of hat that was traditionally worn by the clergy, clerks, lawmakers, and academics. The term, in relation to the sarcastic dimension of the attack of Catderousse and Poulin against d'Opède, directly relates to the fact that even if he is the de facto leader of the royal troops, his men consider him as an intellectual who does not know anything of combat on the field, hence the reflection on law and judgment that comes right after.

[2] "Entendre" does not carry here the meaning of "to hear," but rather that of "focus," "know," "rely."

[3] D'Opède is here being criticized for his law-oriented decisions. He may know, as Catderousse implies, many things about the different forms of punishment that a convict may be sentenced to, but he does not know about the reality of war, how it happens on the battlefield, as Poulin explains in the following line.

Catderousse
Si nous eussions suivy & et redoublé l'assaut
N'eussions nous pas franchi le rempar de plain saut
N'eussions nous pas desia l'enseigne sur la bresche

Poulin
Nos ennemys voyans que rien ne les empesche
Ont seurement leur lieu Imprenable rendu
Et nous l'avons couards trop lachement perdu

Aj

*Tragedy of the Sack of Cabrières*

Catderousse
If we had continued the assault and doubled our efforts,
Wouldn't we already have leapt over their ramparts?
Wouldn't we already have raised our flag on their breached walls?

Poulin
Our enemies, seeing that nothing could stop them,
Have surely made their place impregnable
And we, cowards, have shamefully abandoned it!

[2r]

Catderousse 2
Quiconque se veoit chef d'une puissante armée
S'il a profond au cœur la vertu imprimée
Iamais fortifier ne laisse l'Ennemi

Poulin
Si du tout il ne peut il le rompt à demi
Tantost par fausse alarme & tantost de grand force
L'assaut à l'improviste & rudement le force

Catderousse
Le Cœur glacé de peur ne sait jamais pouvoir

Poulin
Ô le grand bien que c'est que de rien ne savoir[1]
L'homme le plus rusé en proces & querele
En la guerre n'eut onc une once de cervelle

D'Opède
Bien qu'homme je ne soye à nul de vous pareil
En force & hardiesse, aussi peu qu'en conseil
Les Conseils de la main en moy pourtant se treuvent
Tels que quelques amys quelqueffois les appreuvent.

Catderousse
Qui vous empesche donc ayant si bons souldars
D'encor les hazarder au dernier sort de Mars?

---

[1] The line starts with a large hand-drawn o.

*Tragedy of the Sack of Cabrières* 53

[2r]

Catderousse
Whoever sees himself as the leader of a powerful army,
If valor is deeply engraved in his heart,
Would never let the enemy grow strong.[1]

Poulin
If he cannot fully destroy his enemy, at least he must half break him,
Now with false alarms, now with brute force
He must assault them unexpectedly, and roughly subdue them.

Catderousse
He whose heart is frozen by fear knows not how to think and act.[2]

Poulin
How good it is not to know anything!
The cleverest man in trials and quarrels
Has not an ounce of brain in the affairs of war!

D'Opède
Even though as a man I am like neither of you,
In strength, boldness, or in counsel,
Nevertheless, the advice I devise still
Sometimes finds approval among my friends.

Catderousse
What is then holding you back, with such good mercenaries,
From sending them to cast their lot with Mars?[3]

---

[1] Another attack against d'Opède; this is specifically what he should be doing as their leader.

[2] "Pouvoir" here is to be considered in an intellectual, not physical sense; the translation with "think and act" carries the idea that fear, when a leader experiences it, annihilates his possibility to act. This is, once again, the continuation of the ridiculing of d'Opède's actions, and even legitimacy, by his men.

[3] Mars, the god of war. Catderousse here wonders why d'Opède does not use their skilled army to attack the city. The reference to the god, famous for his impatience and violence, and the term "souldars" (soldiers for hire) underline the vision of Catderousse on the situation. Extreme violence, at the cost of many lives, is for him the solution to end the siege. This violent stance of the officer is further developed later on, and is hinted throughout the whole play.

D'Opède
Un songe nuit & jour dormant veillant me bride
Par l'exemple fameux de la chaine d'Alcide
Delaquelle il tira vers luy prompts les Gauloys
Par l'oreille enyvrez du doux miel de sa voix
Tout ainsi ceste ville à ma langue attachée
Me semble tomber bas d'elle mesme arrachée

Aij

D'Opède
A dream that I have night and day restrains me:
Just like Alcides[1] with his chain,
With which he brought the Gauls to him,[2]
And seduced them with the sweet honey of his voice,
This very city, seduced by my words,
Will fall down, destroyed by my tongue.

---

[1] Heracles. From Ἀλκείδης, the name originally given to him to mark his relation to his ancestor Alcaeus (Ἀλκαῖος), son of Perseus and Andromeda.

[2] This reference is an allusion to the image of the "Hercule gaulois," the Gallic Hercules, particularly important in the Renaissance. Geoffroy Tory, in *Champfleury* (1529), develops the idea of an aging Hercules, whose main weapon is now the power of his words. Tory, including in his work his own translation of Lucian's *Heracles*, explains that "Hercules tire après luy une merveilleuse grande multitude d'hommes et de femmes, tous atachés l'ung à part de l'autre par l'oreille. Les liens estoient *petites chaînes d'or et d'ambre bien faictes* ... tous *alègres et joyeulx le suyvent* en eulx émerveillant de luy" (Hercules draws toward him a marvelously great multitude of men and women, all bound to each other by the ear. The links are *well-crafted small chains of gold and amber.* ... They all *follow him, joyous and happy*, and are amazed by him; italics mine). Geoffroy Tory, *Champfleury*, ed. J. L. Joliffe (New York: Johnson Reprint, 1970), Biii.

[2v]

Mon DEVIN[1] sur cela enquis m'a respondu
De les vouloir forcer ce n'est que temps perdu
La lance n'y peust rien mais seulement la langue.

Poulin
I'ay fait devant le Turc mainte fausse harangue
Et si l'ay mainteffois par mon faulx doux parler
Contraint de cinq cens naux faire sur mer voler
Ses Bacchats s'efforceoient de tout m'y contredire
Je l'emportoy pourtant bravement par mon dire.

Catderousse
"Mais qui a un bon cœur & les armes au poin[2]
"Du babil de la langue il n'a aucun besoin

D'Opede
"La langue (croyez) prend et ravit plus de ville
"Que la pique ou canon ne tous efforts hostiles.

---

[1] In all caps in the manuscript.

[2] In sixteenth-century printed theater texts, unclosed quotation marks indicate that what follows is a maxim, a proverb, or a saying, not direct discourse or quotation.

# [2v]

When asked about this, my SEER told me
That it was wasted effort to try to coerce them.
The spear cannot help us, only words will.[1]

Poulin
I delivered many false speeches to the Turk myself.[2]
Often, with fickle, sweet words,
I compelled him to fly five hundred vessels[3] on the sea.
Although his pashas[4] tried hard to contest my ideas,
I was, however, thanks to my bold speech, victorious.

Catderousse
"But whoever is bold and has weapons in hand
"Has no need of a babbling tongue.

D'Opède
"Words (believe me) take and subdue many more cities
"Than spears, artillery, or hostile force.

---

[1] "Langue" here must be understood as the power of speaking, the power of language, that surpasses that of violence and weapons. The opposition between arms and letters was a recurrent debate of the Renaissance period. See notably James J. Supple, *Arms vs. Letters: The Military and Literary Ideals in the "Essays" of Montaigne* (Oxford: Clarendon Press, 1984).

[2] The use of the singular ("le Turc") creates a symbolic image of a man representing the power and might of the whole Ottoman Empire, as well as offering the quintessential image of the heretic. I would argue that this term could also refer to the sultan of the empire, thus making Poulin, in his repeated effort to ridicule d'Opède, a force of nature who was able to trump the powerful leader.

[3] The word "naux" used here has the specificity of having a different meaning whether it is used in the feminine or in the masculine. Aymar de Raçonnet, *Thrésor de la langue françoyse, tant ancienne que moderne* (Paris: Douceur, 1606) associates "nau" and "navire" and specifies that in the masculine, it means "round sea vessel," whereas in the feminine, it means "a sea army, several vessels assembled together to form an army." It is the feminine meaning that I used here.

[4] The word used in the text, "Bacchats," is a francization of "pasha," itself coming from the Turkish "paşa" meaning "Turkish officer of high rank, as a military commander or a provincial governor" (*Oxford English Dictionary*).

Catderousse
"Une bonne entreprise on ne doit retarder

D'opede
Bien mais apres faudra la langue hazarder
De moy en attendant l'incertain de fortune
Ie me retire a part sans compaignie aucune

Poulin
Quel chef! que gouverneur! quel hardi combattant
Qui iusqu'à veoir ses gens en bataille n'attend
Mais sur tous les poltron le poltron est si lache
Qu'en lieu des premiers estre il s'enfuit et se cache

Catderousse
Pensez qu'ainsi faisoit le superbe vainqueur
Duquel un monde seul ne contentoit le cœur.

Poulin
Allons poulser nos gens que ces forts on canõne.[1]

---

[1] One of the very few examples where the nasalization of the diphthong is shown with a tilde.

*Tragedy of the Sack of Cabrières* 59

Catderousse
"One should never delay a good operation.

D'Opède
Certainly, but one must afterwards venture what words can do.
However, while I wait for this uncertain fortune,
I depart, alone and with no company.

Poulin
What a leader! What a governor! What a bold warrior,
Who does not even stay to watch his men fight!
Of all cowards, the most cowardly is he
Who, instead of being on the front lines would rather run and hide!

Catderousse
Consider that the proud victor,
For whom one world was not enough, did the same.[1]

Poulin
Let us spur our troops to bombard these forts!

---

[1] The "superbe vainqueur" in question is Alexander the Great (356–323 BC). His gigantic empire covered a territory spanning from modern-day Greece to the Himalayas. Alexander was famous in the Renaissance as a great conqueror and king, and one of the most powerful warriors ever. He was used in many didactic and historical books as a model of strength to be followed. See Corinne Jouanno, ed., *Figures d'Alexandre à la Renaissance* (Turnhout: Brepols, 2012).

[3r]

Catderousse 3
Que le dernier assaut de toutes pars on donne

Poulin
Ou vivons y vainqueurs ou mourons y vaincuz

Catderousse
Si nous n'y entrons vifs mourons sous nos escus.

## LE CHŒUR
Du sac de Merindol cruellement funeste
Troupe captive au Camp de ces brigans je reste.
Les autres sont heureux qui errent par les champs
Encor plus heureux sont ceux à qui ces meschans
Ont esteint les tormens en esteignant la vie
La nostre a petit feu nous doit estre ravie
Si faut il constament tenir pour resolu
Que c'est pour nostre bien puis que DIEU[1] l'a voulu.
Cabriere cependant redouble son courage
Et d'Opede affoibli de plus en plus enrage
"Pource que contre Dieu n'y a force ne conseil[2]
"Qu'il ne desrompe ainsi que les nerfs d'un sommeil
Comme ces assiegez travaillent tous ensemble!
Ce gros amas de peuple aux abeilles ressemble
Lesquelles pour se faire à part nouveau canton
S'entresuivent au son d'un clairsonnant laitton.
Ou quand pour reparer leur utile dommage

---

[1] In all caps in the manuscript.
[2] See [2v] note 2.

*Tragedy of the Sack of Cabrières*                                                     61

[3r]

Catderousse
Let us assault from all sides one last time!

Poulin
Let us either live as victors or die here vanquished!

Catderousse
May we die with our shields in hand if we cannot enter the city alive!

THE CHORUS
From the cruel and deadly sack of Mérindol,
A captive troop we remain in the camp of these brigands.
Happy are those who wander in the fields;
Even happier are those whose torments
Were extinguished by these villains, when they took their lives;
As for us, our lives must be taken by slow fire.[1]
However, we must constantly be assured that
This is for our own good, since GOD has willed it.[2]
Meanwhile, Cabrières redoubles its courage,
And d'Opède, weakened, rages more and more.
"Since for God, there is no force or counsel
"That he cannot break, as anxiety breaks sleep.
See how these besieged men labor together!
This great cluster of men resembles bees
Who, in order to build their new canton,[3]
Together follow a clear-sounding horn.[4]
Thus, when they aim to repair the damages

---

[1] A form of torture and execution combined by which a victim is slowly roasted to death, rather than quickly burned (see "Of Coaches" by Michel de Montaigne, in which he describes the torture and death of the king of Mexico). Théodore Agrippa d'Aubigné, in "Les Feux," uses the same reference: "La mort à petit feu lui ôte son écorce" (Fire slowly burns his skin and kills him). Théodore Agrippa d'Aubigné, *Les Tragiques,* ed. Frank Lestringant (Paris: Gallimard, 2003), 198. I thank Kathleen Long for pointing to the connections between the play and *Les Tragiques,* published almost sixty years later in 1616.

[2] The idea of God testing his flock is central to the Vaudois faith; throughout the text, the numerous exactions that are committed against them, although painful, are seen as trials in order to be accepted into the kingdom to come.

[3] The word "canton" literally meant "corner," "location," "place."

[4] "Clairsonnant laitton" is a metonymy on the metal ("laiton," brass) of which the instrument is made.

Apres qu'on a brisé l'orgueil de leur ouvrage
Toutes devant les yeux de leur Roy honnoré
Chambrittent au compas leur palais tout doré
Un regiment des champs les richesses apporte
Qu'une autre troupe prend & descharge à la porte.

Aiij

*Tragedy of the Sack of Cabrières*                                   63

Caused when their proud work was destroyed,
Before the eyes of their honored king,
They rebuild their golden palace chamber by chamber in good order.[1]
A regiment brings in the bountiful harvest
which another group takes and unloads at the gates.

---

[1] "Chambrittent au compas." Boccassini, in her edition (226, n. 86), argues that this expression, hardly found anywhere else, refers to the geometrical construction of beehives.

[3v]

Maint scadron au dedans les porte sur son flanc
Dont les autres refont leurs sales ranc à ranc
Et ne cesse jamais ceste race aerée
Tant que leur grand maison soit du tout reparée
Ceux de la ville ainsi travaillent aux rempars
La terre sous leurs piez fume de toutes pars
L'un porte des fagots & l'autre force laine
L'autre tant de gazons qu'il en est hors d'alaine
Force pierres ceux cy ceux là force fumier
Cestui cy des grands bois marchant tout le premier
Et ceux là plus hastez y iettent leurs lits mesmes
Mais cestui là y fourre (ô mon Dieu) les corps blesmes
Des leurs souldars occis pour encor s'en servir
Voyez descendre l'un voyez l'autre gravir
À grands coups de mouton les autres tant terrassent
Que leurs rempars levés toute bresche surpassent.
Voyez vous l'ennemy contre le mur courir
Ô Dieu qui es leur fort vueilles les secourir
Dieu par qui à ton peuple estoient defenses faites
De combattre devant que sonner les trompettes.
Nous enseignant par là pour ne combattre en vain
Qu'il faut que nous prenions les armes de ta main

*Tragedy of the Sack of Cabrières*

[3v]

Many squadrons carry it on their flanks,
And others use it to rebuild their rooms, row after row,
And this airy race will never cease its work
Until their great home is completely rebuilt.
Thus, the townspeople work on the ramparts,
The soil under their feet is smoking from all sides.[1]
One brings kindling wood, the other a lot of wool,
Another one so much hay that he is breathless.
These ones here carry many stones, and those over there much manure,
That one marching first brings in big sticks of wood,
And those, very hastily, throw in even their beds![2]
That other man stuffs in (O God!) the pale bodies
Of their dead soldiers, so that they can still serve their city!
Some come down the walls, and some climb them.
With their mallets,[3] they level the ground so well
That the new ramparts are stronger than the ones that were breached.[4]
See the enemy charge against our walls!
O Lord, you who are their fort,[5] we implore you to rescue them!
God through whom the defense of your people was made,
You who instructed them to fight before sounding the trumpets.[6]
Thus, you taught us that in order not to fight in vain,
We must use the weapons you gave to us.

---

[1] The smoking soil ("terre [qui] fume") could be a reference to "terre fumée" or "fumement de terre," a gardening technique consisting of enriching soil with manure (see de Raçonnet, *Thrésor de la langue françoyse*, where it is defined as "stercoratio"). It could also be a reference to the dust made by the trampling of the ground by workers. Both references, however, indicate the same notion of hard work.

[2] These lines show the desperate attempts made by the inhabitants of Cabrières to repair their walls, using any material they can find.

[3] "Mouton," to be understood here as a leveling tool, used to flatten or pierce the soil, rather than in as a battering ram.

[4] Their hard work was able not only to repair the damage done during the last assault, but also to make their walls sturdier than ever.

[5] A probable reference to Martin Luther's "Ein feste Burg ist unser Gott" ("A Mighty Fortress Is Our God"), one of his most famous hymns.

[6] A reference to the seven trumpets that will be sounded by the angels after the seventh seal is broken during the Apocalypse, as described in Rev. 8:2, 5–6: "And I saw the seven angels who stand before God, and to them were given seven trumpets / … Then the angel took the censer, filled it with fire from the altar, and threw it to the earth. And there were noises, thunderings, lightnings, and an earthquake. / So the seven angels who had the seven trumpets prepared themselves to sound."

Arme donques les tiens d'une hardiesse sainte
Et saisi ces meschans d'une mortelle crainte
Qu'ils ne soyent jamais veus de ce lieu triomphans
Pour avoir massacré ô Pere tes enfans

D'opede
Est il donc arresté qu'une heure en patience
Vivre ne me lairras maudite conscience
Pourquoy veux je ce peuple estre tout massacré

*Tragedy of the Sack of Cabrières*

So, arm your people with holy boldness
And fill the villains with deadly fear,
So that they are never seen victorious in this place,
They who massacred, O Father, your children.

D'Opède
Is it determined, then, that you will never
Leave me alone an hour, oh you wretched conscience?
Why do I want all of these people to be massacred?

[4r]

Ce peuple tout fidele et à Dieu consacré!                    4
Ce peuple dont la vie est si saintement pure
Que pour l'amour de luy Dieu encor nous endure
France seroit en proye & les François captifs
Ou serviroient au Turc ou esclaves craintifs
Seroient ja transportez au profond des Hespaignes
Sans le vœu d'oraison que fait en ces montaignes
Ce saint tropeau tousiours pour le Roy exaucé
Que fera donc ce camp qu'ici ie tiens dressée?
Le ciel leur favorise & m'est de tout contraire
Dieu prend leur cause en main & ie les veux defaire
Si faut il passer outre ou mourir ou je suis
Desister je ne veux & aussi je ne puis
"Car l'homme qui du tout acheve un meschant acte
"N'apparoit si meschant qu'un sot qui s'en retracte
"Cestui cy luy mesme est le Juge de son fait
"Pource le condamnant qu'il le laisse imparfait
"Mais l'autre qui poursuyt jusqu'à la fin son œuvre
"Semble estre vertueux quand tout son mal il coeuvre
"D'une perseverance entiere sous espoir
"D'une agreable issue a ses desirs avoir
Ô que si jamais donc je romps mon entreprise
La roüe d'Ixion pour Ixion me brise

[4r]

This faithful people, wholly devoted to God!
This people, whose life is so blessedly pure,
That for their love God still tolerates us?
France would be prey, and all the French captives
Would either serve the Turks or be taken
To farthest Spain as fearful slaves
Without the prayers that this holy people offer in these mountains,[1]
Prayers always granted for the king.[2]
I have this camp in readiness; what will it do?
The heavens are with them and are completely opposed to me!
God is taking their cause in hand, and I want to destroy them!
Then, I must either see this through, or die on the spot;
I do not want to stand down, and nor can I.
"For a man who carries out a bad action to its completion
"Does not appear as evil as the fool who recants.
"He himself is the judge of his own actions,
"And when he condemns them, he leaves them unfinished.
"But the other, who pursues his work until the end
"Seems virtuous when he covers his evil
"With full perseverance, hoping that
"His desires will have a favorable end.[3]
May I, if I ever abandon this endeavor,
Be broken like Ixion was on his wheel![4]

---

[1] The Luberon Massif, in southern France, the region in which Cabrières is located, east of Avignon.

[2] The Vaudois respected the authority of the king and were not violently against the monarchy; they were not, then, enemies of the state, as Catderousse and Poulin argue.

[3] The rhetoric of d'Opède is following a hard line. His transformation is complete with this demonstration. Indeed, he would rather convince himself that his bad actions could have a positive side than cover himself with shame by accepting that he is wrong. The old d'Opède is definitely gone, as are his doubts, replaced by the cruel, cold-hearted new leader.

[4] In Greek mythology, Ixion was particularly deceitful character. After killing his father-in-law Deioneus, because Ixion did not want to give him the fabulous treasure he had promised should he let Ixion marry his daughter, he was punished by the gods and condemned to madness. Zeus had pity on him and invited him to Olympus, where he started to try to seduce Hera. Furious, Zeus expelled him, struck him with lightning, and had him bound to a fiery wheel. See Sophocles, *Phyloctetes,* vv. 678–83, trans. P. Meineck and P. Woodruff (Indianapolis: Hackett, 2007): "I once heard a story, though I never saw it myself / Of one who dared to try to bed the wife of Zeus. / He was caught by Cronus' mighty son / And lashed to the rim of an ever-running wheel. / But I have never seen or

Que me serviroit il qu'au lieu d'un bonnet rond
De cest armet doré ie me couvre le front?
Au lieu de ma grand robbe avoir ceste cuirasse?
Pour la plume en la main ceste pesante masse?
Suis je quictant ma mule armé sur ce roussin
Pour m'enfuir en lieu d'attendre & veoir la fin
Ay ie bruslé Pepin la Motte Saint Estienne

Aiiij

*Tragedy of the Sack of Cabrières* 71

What use would it be to have, rather than by a scholar's cap,
My forehead adorned by a golden helm?
What use to wear this armor, rather than my long robe,
And hold in my hand this heavy mace rather than my quill?
Am I leaving my mule behind, going off armed on my warhorse[1]
To decamp, instead of waiting to see how things end?
Have I burned to the ground Pépin, La Motte, Saint-Etienne,

---

heard of any mortal / Suffering a more hateful fate than this man." By deliberately comparing himself to Ixion, d'Opède emphasizes the dimension of no return in his decision to destroy Cabrières. Should he change his mind, his punishment would be as harsh as that of the Thessalian.

[1] The "roussin" in question is a valueless horse, used by knights to learn how to mount, and for work in the field. They were neither elegant nor expensive, but were considered to be good for carrying heavily armed men, as Randle Cotgrave explains in his *Dictionarie of the French and English Tongues* (see http://www.pbm.com/~lindahl/cotgrave/838small.html).

[4v]

Lormarin, Valelaure & la Roche prochaine
Foudroyé Cabrierette abysmé Merindol
Saccagé Saint Martin ay je ravi d'un vol
Vingt bourgs villes chasteaux les ay mis en braise
Comme n'ayans servi iamais que de fournaise
Ay je donques destruit tant d'hommes & de lieux
Pour estre pitoyable en lieu de furieux
Afin qu'en espargnant ce reste de Canailles
Ie leur quicte le fruit de toutes mes batailles
Seroit ce bien à fin que ce que j'ay gaigné
Soit à mon ennemy pour l'avoir espargné!
Et qu'on dist de D'Opede il obtient bien victoire
Mais il n'en scait user à son profit ne gloire
Je les ay condamnez à perdre biens & corps
Qu'ils ne vivent donc plus ils m'enrichissent morts
Sus sus sus que pour moy leur arrest j'exequute
Ceste grand'Courtisane à qui mon bien j'impute
Ayant de don du Roy leur confiscation
M'a fait pour petit pris de son droit cession
Avec tout plain pouvoir de lever des gendarmes
Gens de pied et souldars bien exercez aux armes
Enseignes desployer estendars, gomphanons
Mener artillerie & braquer gros Canons
Voilà comme ie suis general capitaine
De tout ce camp lequel où il me plait ie meine

[4v]

Lourmarin, Valelaure, and La Roche,
Have I struck down Cabrierette,[1] have I ruined Mérindol,[2]
Sacked Saint Martin, have I ransacked
Twenty villages, towns, or castles, have I turned them to ashes,
As if they were never anything but furnaces,
Have I then destroyed so many men and places
To be pitiful instead of furious,
So that, by sparing this despicable rabble,
I yield to them the fruit of my battles?
Would it be fair, in the end, that what I gained
Belonged to my enemy, because I spared him,
So that one might say of d'Opède: "vanquish, he did,
But he did not profit or get glory from it."
I sentenced them to lose their lives and their goods;
May they stop living! Their deaths will make me rich![3]
Die, Die, Die! I shall enforce their sentence!
This great courtesan, to whom I impute my wealth,[4]
Offered me, for a decent price, cession of her right
That she obtained through confiscation by the king.
I have all power to hire men at arms,
Foot soldiers, and mercenaries skilled in arms.
Raise the flags, the standards, the banners,
Bring the artillery, and aim the cannons:
This is how I am the general and captain
Of this whole camp, which I lead wherever I please.

---

[1] This is most definitely a different writing of "Cabrières," according to Jacques Aubéry, as he explains in his edition of the *Histoire de l'execution de Cabrières et de Mérindol et d'autres lieux de Provence,* ed. Gabriel Audisio (Paris: Éditions de Paris, 1990). This form can also be found in the proceedings of the trial: "A Cabrierette, il y eut quatre hommes tués" (107).

[2] All these villages are located in the vicinity of Cabrières.

[3] The reference to material wealth is present throughout the play; the author reinforces through it the fact that the actions of the Catholics are not even motivated by their desire to defend their religion or to obey the king, but rather by pure greed, a sin severely condemned notably by Aquinas, who noted in the *Summa Theologica* (2–2, Question 118) that it was "a sin against God, just as all mortal sins, in as much as man condemns things eternal for the sake of temporal things." See New Advent, http://www.newadvent.org/summa/3118.htm.

[4] The church. The imagery of lechery is often associated with the Catholic Church in Protestant literature. The courtesan in question here could very likely be the Whore of Babylon, whose power turns d'Opède from righteousness to evil.

Tous mourront du premier iusques au dernier ranc
Ou je mettray Cabriere au jour d'huy toute en sang.

## LE CHŒUR
L'eternel a ouy nostre ardante priere
Faisant que ces vilains ont tourné le derrière

*Tragedy of the Sack of Cabrières*

They will all die, from the first to the last ranks,
Or today I will cover Cabrières all in blood.

THE CHORUS
The Eternal heard our ardent prayer,
For these villains have retreated![1]

---

[1] The original expression underlines the fact that their bottom ("derrière") can be seen as they left, as they turned their back on the attack.

[5r]

Catderousse & D'opede                                          5

Catderousse
Nos ennemys nous ont si vaillans repoussez
Qu'ils ont de nos gens morts remplis tous leurs fossés
Poulin à cest'heure est pour vous tenir promesse
Avecques un heraut pres de leur forteresse
Nous voicy vostre gendre & saint Romain aussi
Et autres principaux qui retournons icy
Nous avons d'un accord par Poulin fait la treve
Attendant que couvert son œuvre il paracheve
Il a ia fait sortir les gouverneurs vers luy
Croyez qu'il les rendra captifs dans ce jour d'huy.

D'Opede
Si Poulin envers moy ne se monstre fidele
La peine de la mort ne m'est assés cruelle
Ô jour trop malheureux! quelles gens se sont mis
Pour renfort dans la ville avec nos ennemis

Catderousse
Autres qu'eux n'ont defaut tant de nos vaillans hommes

*Tragedy of the Sack of Cabrières*  77

[5r]

Catderousse and D'Opède

Catderousse
Our enemies have so valiantly repelled us
That they have filled the moats of their fortress with the dead soldiers.
To live up to his pledge, Poulin went just now
With a herald to their fortress.
Here we are, with your son-in-law[1] and Saint-Romain,[2]
As well as other leaders who are returning.
We agreed through Poulin to call a truce,
While he treacherously[3] tries to accomplish his deeds.
He already succeeded in having the leaders come out to meet him;
Be assured that he will have taken them prisoner this very day.

D'Opède
Should Poulin be unfaithful to me,[4]
The death penalty will not be cruel enough.
O, most desperate day! Which people came
To reinforce the city, in league with our enemies?

Catderousse
No others have defeated so many of our valiant men.

---

[1] Jean-Anthoine Piton-Curt's *Histoire de la noblesse du comté-Venaissin d'Avignon et de la Principauté d'Orange, dressée sur les preuves, dédiée au Roy* (Paris: David et Delormel, 1763) draws up a chronology of the Meynier family. D'Opède had two daughters from his first union with Louise de Vintimile: Claire Mainier, who married Antoine de Glandevez, Vicomte de Porrieres, and Anne Mainier, who married François Perruzi, Baron of Lauris (2:234–35). The "gendre" in question could then be either of them. It is interesting to note that Balthazar de Maynier's *Histoire de la principale noblesse de Provence* (Aix-en-Provence: Joseph David, 1719) names his first wife: Jean de Maynier Baron d'Oppede […] fut marié avec Anne de Vintimille des Vicomtes de Marseille." (194).

[2] "Louis d'Ancezune-Cadart, Seigneur de Vénéjan, de S. Roman de Malegarde & de S.Estienne" (Piton-Curt, *Histoire de la noblesse du comté-Venaissin*, 52). This man was the brother of Jean d'Ancezune-Cadart, Lord of Catderousse, the historic inspiration for the character of the play.

[3] "Couvert" has a double meaning here of "hidden," to emphasize the covert operations of Poulin, but also "treacherous," which I chose for the translation.

[4] A reference to the treachery of Poulin, foreshadowing his double-crossing of d'Opède later on after his conversion.

D'opede
Contr'un d'eux neantmoins vingt ou trente nous sommes.

Catderousse
Le plus foible souvent surmonte le plus fort

D'opede
Ainsi ballotte Mars le hazard de son sort

Catderousse
Touteffois comme ayant en ma main la victoire
I'enflamboy nos souldars ainsi du feu de gloire
Souldars si vous avez tels cœurs qu'aveiez devāt
Ils sont vaincus c'est fait piquez donques avant
Le premier qui mettra les piez sur la muraille
Aura outre l'honneur ceste riche medaille
Et le second aura ma chaine de pur or
Bj

D'Opède
We are, however, twenty or thirty strong against them.

Catderousse
The weaker often overcomes the stronger.

D'Opède
Thus does Mars balance the chance of fate.[1]

Catderousse
As I am certain we will be victorious,
I set our soldiers ablaze with the fire of glory:
"Soldiers! If your hearts are as strong as they once were,
They will be beaten for sure! So, forward! Spur your horses onward!
The first of you who sets foot on their walls
Will earn, besides honor, this richly adorned medal,
And he who comes next, my chain made of pure gold!

---

[1] Another reference to Mars, the god of war, whose protection or lack thereof may provide success or defeat in battle.

[5v]

Le troisiesme un beau pris & le quatriesme encor
Harquebusiers tirez vous trainans sur le ventre
Poulin, crioit aussi: si le soleil y entre
N'y entrerons nous pas? Courage la dedans
Les poltrons prient Dieu comme ja se rendans
Je crie au canonnier qu'il redouble la bresche
Qu'est du jour d'hyer encore toute fresche
À grands coups de canon qu'il batte leurs rempars
Et ceux qui sont dessus fonçe de toutes pars
Mais un plus asseuré nostre Canonnier perse
Par le milieu du corps & tout mort le renverse
De tout nostre Scadron qui se serroit de pres
Les plus forts sont blessés & repoulsez apres
Si dru ne chet la gresle au giron de la Terre
Comme tombent espés nous vaillans gens de guerre
Panisse alors crioit: comment vous reculez
Et si en avez tant massacrés & bruslés
Bon cœur souldart bon cœur sus entre monte tue
Cependant qu'un chascun combattant s'esvertue
Ce Canonnier nous bat sans cesse & si adroit
Qu'il ne pourroit faillir quand faillir il voudroit

*Tragedy of the Sack of Cabrières*  81

[5v]

The third and the fourth will also earn great prizes.
Harquebusiers,[1] shoot your weapons, flat on your stomachs!"
Poulin was shouting too: "If the sun can enter the city,
Can we not as well? Have courage in there!"
The cowards already pray God, as if they surrender already.
I call for the gunner to widen the breach,
Still open from yesterday's attacks.
May he crush their ramparts with blows from his cannons,
And mow down the men standing on them!
But a bolder man, just pierced the chest of
Our gunner, and knocked him over, dead!
Of our whole squadron, walking in close formation,
The strongest men are injured and pushed back.
Hail does not fall as hard on the ground[2]
As swords fell on our valiant warriors.
Then Panisse[3] shouted: "Why are you retreating?
You have massacred and burned so many already!
Courage, soldiers, courage! Down with them! Get in, climb the walls, kill!"
Meanwhile, as everybody is striving to fight,
Their gunner hit us endlessly and so skillfully
That he could never miss, even if he wished to.

---

[1] The harquebusiers were a kind of light cavalry, generally put in the lines to prepare for the arrival of heavier cavalry. They were generally armed with short swords and an arquebus (harquebus), a limited-range, muzzle-loaded early carbine. However, since these weapons were heavy, and most often required a hook-shaped stand to stabilize them and fire them, it seems unlikely that the troops referred to as such are on horseback in the play. They must have been, instead, infantry troops (which would also complement the reference to cannon below).

[2] Even though it is not presented as such, the beginning of the sentence ("dru ne chet la gresle") is recognized as a proverb by James W. Hassell, Jr. in his *Middle French Proverbs, Sentences, and Proverbial Phrases* (Toronto: Pontifical Institute of Mediaeval Studies, 1982), 130.

[3] The only reference to a Panisse can be found in the 1906 edition of the *Mémoires de l'Académie de Nimes* (Nimes: Clavel et Chastanier, 1906). In the *Extrait des mémoires et livres de raison des Merles de Beauchamp*, written in a Provençal dialect, there is an account of the massacre of Cabrières, with the preparations of the battle, and notably the technical details of the number of pieces of artillery and men; among them can be found "six piesses dartillerie et deus cens hommes que Moss. Le prevost Panisse avoit levé en seste ville" (29). The reference in the next paragraph is to "le capitaine Pollin lequel estoit audavant de Cabrieros et Moss. Le président de Provenso, Moss. D'Oubedo."

Tout ce qu'on a escrit des cent mains de Briaire
Et cent bouches à feu est chose trop vulgaire
Au pris de cestui cy qui tirant bas & haut
Ne cesse de tuer tant que dure l'assaut
Pour les cent mains de l'autre et cent bouche ou forges
Cestui à mille bras & mille ardentes gorges
Dont il vomit le feu si espés foudroyans
Qu'en routte & fuite il met le reste de nos gens
Mais quoy pour eviter une entiere defaite
Ils n'ont point attendu qu'on sonnast la retraite

*Tragedy of the Sack of Cabrières*                                                    83

All the things written about the hundred hands of Briaeros[1]
And the hundred mouths of fire are of no match for this man,
Who, shooting high and low,
Does not stop killing, as long as the battle rages on.
For Briaeros's hundred hands and for his hundred mouths or forges
He has a thousand arms, and also a thousand burning throats
With which he vomits a thick, blasting fire
That makes the rest of our people flee the rout.
But, what? To prevent an utter defeat,
They did not even wait for us to sound the retreat.

---

[1] Briaeros was one of the hecatoncheires, children of Ouranos and Gaia, whom Zeus tasked with the protection of Tartarus. They each had fifty heads and a hundred arms.

[6r]

D'opede

"L'experience auz fols mais c'est trop tard apprend                     6
"Qu'avant le coup le sage & conseil prend
"Qui peut estre vainqueur sans hazarder sa vie
"S'il la hazarde il n'a de la garder envie
Mais puis que Poulin est allé parlementer
À eux devant le temps ne le faut tourmēter
Durant la treve allons au tour de la muraille
Prenans garde que nul de ces meschants n'en saille.
Car i'ay iuré que vif nul n'en eschappera
Hommes femmes enfans tout meurtry y sera

Catderousse

Adieu donc car Poulin aux vilains fait entendre
Que Je veux contre vous pour eux les armes prendre

Le Chœur

La victoire
Ne vient pas
Ne la gloire! par le pas
Ni compas
Du mortel
L'immortel
Qui l'ordonne
Seul la donne

De nature l'escorce est
Bien peu dure

Bij

*Tragedy of the Sack of Cabrières*　　　　　　　　　　　　85

[6r]

D'Opède
"Experience teaches the fools, but now it is too late,
"That before the attack, the wise man seeks advice.[1]
"He who can be victorious without risking his life
"Does not wish to be saved, if he still exposes it.
But since Poulin is off to parley with them,
We should not worry too soon.
During this break, let us gather around the fort;
Take care that none of them sallies forth.
For I swore that no one would escape alive
Men, women, or children: all will be massacred!

Catderousse
Farewell, then! Poulin is letting the villains hear
That I want to take arms for them against you.

The Chorus
Victory
Does not come,
And neither does glory, through the steps
Within the compass
Of mortal men.
The Immortal,
Who orders it,
Is the only one who grants it.[2]

By its nature, the bark of a tree
Is not very hard,

---

[1] See Prov. 20:18: "Plans are established by counsel; by wise counsel wage war."
[2] Maybe a reference to Ps. 62:7: "In God is my salvation and my glory; the rock of my strength, and my refuge, is in God."

[6v]

La forest
Pourtant naist
S'espessit
Se grossit
Et renforce
Sous lescorce

L'arbre elle arme
Contre l'air
Et l'alarme
Rouge & clair
De l'esclair
Pour le fruit
Qu'il produit
De fleurs belles
Annuelles.

De l'escaille
L'ast de mer
Fait sa maille
Pour s'armer
Et de l'äer
Les legiers
Chevaliers
Font rondeles
De leurs ailes.

*Tragedy of the Sack of Cabrières*  87

[6v]

Yet the forest
Does emerge,
Flourishes,
Grows,
And strengthens
Under the bark.

It arms the tree
Against the air,
And against the menace
Red and bright
Of the lightning strike;
For the fruit
It produces,
From the annual bloom
Of beautiful flowers.

From its scales
The lobster[1]
Makes an armor
To protect himself.
From the air,
The swift woodcocks[2]
Make a shield
From their wings.

---

[1] Boccassini argues that the "ast de mer" is a crayfish. However, I consider that this word comes from a direct translation of the Latin "Astacus Marinus," which appears in Guillaume Antoine-Olivier's *Encyclopédie Méthodique* (Paris: Panckouke, 1791) as "ecrevisse homard" (342).

[2] "Chevaliers" here refers to the bird, and obviously not the fighter. See the definition given by Pierre-Charles Berthelin in the *Abrégé du dictionnaire universel françois et latin, vulgairement appellé dictionnaire de Trévoux* (Paris: Libraires associés, 1762), 437: "oiseau aquatique qui a le bec long, et les jambes si hautes, qu'il est comme a cheval, et c'est pour cela qu'on l'appelle chevalier" (an aquatic bird with a long beak, and such long legs that it looks like it is riding a horse, and that is why it is called a knight).

[7r]

La Limasse 7
Dans son fort
Se ramasse
Et n'en sort
Ains tient fort
D'ongles grands
Corne & dens
Mainte beste
Se font teste.

Chasque sorte
En ses droits
Se tient forte
Mais des Rois
Nul harnois
Tant soit fort
Que la mort
Ne les darde
Ne les garde

Quelque ruse
Ou scavoir
Dont l'homme use
Quelque avoir
Ou pouvoir
Qu'il fait sien.
Ce n'est rien
Quand Dieu contre
Fait sa monstre.                    Biij

[7r]

The snail
In its fort
Curls up
And does not budge;
Thus it lives on.
With long claws,
Horns, and teeth,
Many beasts
Are jousting.

Every sort
Onto its right,
Is holding tight.
But for kings,
No armor,
However strong,
Can protect them
From the stings
Of Death.[1]

It exerts
Whatever cunning
Or knowledge
That mankind uses,
Whatever possession
Or power;
They are nothing
When God
Appears in glory against them.

---

[1] The lines in stanzas 2 and 3 of this folio were reorganized in the translation to make it intelligible.

[7v]

Rien le nombre
Des souldars
De l'encombre et hazards
Du dur Mars
Quand Dieu veut
Rien ne peut
Tout en somme
Sauver l'homme

Ains la dextre
Du seul Dieu
Et seul maistre
En tout lieu
Au milieu
Du combat
Seule abbat
Mort sur l'herbe
Le superbe.

Elle seule
À la mer
Fait la geule
Defermer
Puis ramer
A beau pied
Dans le gué
Son armée
Pourchassée

*Tragedy of the Sack of Cabrières*　　　　91

[7v]

Neither the number
Of soldiers,
Nor the obstacles and dangers
Of Mars the harsh one,
When God wills,
Nothing can be done,
Indeed,
To save mankind.

Only the right hand[1]
Of the one and only God,
And only master
Of all places,
In the middle
Of the fight
Strikes to death
The proud,
Outstretched on the grass.

Only that hand[2]
Can open
The mouth
Of the sea,[3]
And bring
To the safety
Of the ford
His hunted down
Army.

---

[1] The reference to the right hand of God will here be present throughout the rest of the speech of the Chorus.

[2] In the original text, the subject of these actions is "la dextre," thus what follows is introduced by the feminine pronoun "elle." However, using "it" would be too vague and would not carry the divine power and presence that the hand of God has in the passage. That is why I decided to translate this occurrence by "that hand," which refers to God himself, doing these actions through the presence of his hand.

[3] A reference to the crossing of the Red Sea: "And Moses stretched out his hand over the sea; and when the morning appeared, the sea returned to its full depth, while the Egyptians were fleeing into it. So the LORD overthrew the Egyptians in the midst of the sea. / Then the waters returned and covered the chariots, the horsemen, and all the army of Pharaoh that came into the sea after them. Not so much as one of them remained" (Exod. 14:27–28).

[8r]

Or l'Egypte 8
Pour cela
Plus s'irrite
Dont par la
Devalla
Au tombeau
Dessous l'eau
Qui l'engorge
Dans sa gorge

La gent sainte
Puis eut peur
D'un camp ceinte
Quand l'horreur
Du Geant
Maugreant
La defie
De sa vie

Elle pleure
Et David
Tout sur l'heure
Elle veit
Qui seul feit
Ce rocher
Trebuscher
Bas à terre d'une pierre

Biiij

*Tragedy of the Sack of Cabrières*

93

[8r]

And Egypt
Because of this
Was even more enraged,
And by his hand
Was thrown
In a tomb
Under water,
And all were flooded
In the pass.[1]

The holy army[2]
Was frightened, then,
Inside its encampment
By the horrible sight
Of the blaspheming
Giant
Making an attempt
On its life.[3]

The army was weeping,
And at that moment,
It saw how
David,
By himself,
Made this rock of a man
Tumble down
On the ground, with a single stone.[4]

---

[1] The death of Pharaoh during the Exodus; since his body was swallowed alongside his army, the sea became his de facto tomb. See Exod. 15:4: "Pharaoh's chariots and his army He has cast into the sea; his chosen captains also are drowned in the Red Sea."

[2] Based on what comes next, "gent" here refers to the army of Israel, before its fight against the Philistines: "And Saul and the men of Israel were gathered together, and they encamped in the Valley of Elah, and drew up in battle array against the Philistines" (1 Sam. 17:2).

[3] The giant in question is obviously Goliath: "And a champion went out from the camp of the Philistines, named Goliath, from Gath, whose height was six cubits and a span" (1 Sam. 17:4).

[4] "Then David put his hand in his bag and took out a stone; and he slung it and struck the Philistine in his forehead, so that the stone sank into his forehead, and he fell on his face to the earth" (1 Sam. 17:49).

[8v]

Qui s'appuye
Au Seigneur
Et s'y fie
Aura l'heur
Et l'honeur
Et le pris
D'avoir pris
Ses contraires
Adversaires

Poulin le Maire le Chœur & le Syndique

Poulin
Ces captifs m'ont suivy. Ils consultent ensemble
J'ay peu d'icy ouyr leurs propos dont je tremble

Le Maire
Celuy qui parlemente à l'ennemy se vend

Le chœur
L'asiégé par l'oreille en la prestant se prend

Le maire
Ce n'est pas en la guerre ou derechef on peche
La premiere faute est une mortelle bresche

Le chœur
La la premiere faute est d'un encombre tel
Qu'amender ne se peut par l'esprit du mortel.

Le maire
Quelle rage vous a privez d'intelligence!

*Tragedy of the Sack of Cabrières*  95

[8v]

Whoever relies
On the Lord
And trusts him
Will have the good fortune,
The honor,
And the reward
To dispose of
His adversaries,
Who were his enemies.

Poulin, the Mayor, the Chorus, and the Syndic[1]

Poulin
These captives have followed me. They take counsel with each other
And, trembling, I can hear them speaking from here.

The Mayor
He who parleys with the enemy is selling himself.[2]

The Chorus
But the besieged, who gives his ear, surrenders himself.

The Mayor
One should not blunder while at war;
The first mistake opens a deadly breach.

The Chorus
The original sin is of such importance,
That the deeds of the mortal cannot undo it.

The Mayor
What rage deprived you of your wits!

---

[1] "Syndique" refers here to the notion of city magistrate, as stated in de Raçonnet, *Thrésor de la langue françoyse*, 613: "Syndic, et Procureur d'une Communauté, Actor vniuersitatis, Syndicus." The syndic, then, represented the inhabitants of a locality to the suzerain. The fact that the mayoral officers in Geneva are called "syndiques" or "syndics" also gives a nod to the reformist origin of the play. I will then translate this notion by "syndic," its most direct and logical acceptance. The meaning of property management agent, the most common in modern French, came later.

[2] Montaigne, in his "Si le chef d'une place assiégée doit sortir pour parlementer" [Whether the governor himself goes out to parley] (*Essais*, book I, chapter 5) examines this issue.

[9r]

Quelle fureur vous oste insensés cognoissance!         9
Qui vous a hors du sens si brutalement mis
Que de capituler avec nos ennemis!

Le Chœur
Si Cabriere en avoit encore dix semblables
Ses murailles seroient pour iamais imprenables
L'appas & trahison de l'endormant flateur
Sans leur nuire cherroit sur le chef de l'autheur

Le maire
Estimeriez vous bien que vers vous Poulin sorte
De ce gouffre d'Opede & qu'il vous en apporte
Mot qui ne soit le fiel de douloureuse mort

Poulin
C'est fait de moy c'est fait je suis pris je suis mort.

Le maire
N'apercevez vous point le venin de d'opede!
Ou bien l'appercevant ny mettez vous remede
Helas cognoissez vous si peu ce faux Poulin
Ce faux Poulin remply du faux esprit malin
Ce faux Poulin duquel les Turcs sont les nourrices
Ce faux Poulin qui fait de toutes vertus vices
Ce faux Poulin qui croit en Dien comm'un cheval
Le meschant (croyez moy) nostre ruyne forge
Venant pour nous couper des nos cousteaux la gorge

Le Syndique
"Quand d'esperer la paix quelqu' heureux signe luit
"Sedition n'a lieu qu'entre les furieux

Cj

# [9r]

What furor impaired your common sense, oh you fools!
Who made you lose your sense so much that
You surrender to our enemies!

The Chorus
If Cabrières had ten men like him,
Its walls would be forever impregnable.
The seduction and treachery of the seducing flatterer,[1]
Then, would not harm them, but fall back on him.

The Mayor
Would you accept if Poulin brought d'Opède
From this abyss to you, and if he brought with him
The venomous promise of an impeding death?

Poulin
I am finished, I am discovered, I am dead!

The Mayor
Can you not feel the poison of d'Opède!
Or, if you do, are you not trying to remedy it?
Alas! Do you not recognize this deceitful Poulin?
This deceitful Poulin, swollen with a duplicitous and malevolent spirit,
This deceitful Poulin, who was nurtured by the Turks,
This deceitful Poulin, who makes all virtues vices,
This deceitful Poulin, who believes in God like a horse,[2]
This villain (do believe me!) forges our ruin,
And he is coming to slit our throats with our own knives!

The Syndic
"When hope for peace shines on the horizon,
"Only men mad with violence talk of sedition.

---

[1] "Endormant" here is to be understood as an agent whose actions symbolically put people off guard, in order to destroy them more easily.

[2] Possible reference to Ps. 32:9, "Do not be like the horse or like the mule, / Which have no understanding, / Which must be harnessed with bit and bridle, / Else they will not come near you."

[9v]

Pourtant doit l'eviter quiconque sa charrue
Veut veoir de halecrets en coutres revestue
Maire retirez vous pour n'empescher tel heur

Le maire
C'est bien dit, car la mort aux Chrestiens n'est malheur

Le chœur
Le feu celeste rapt qu'on feint de Promethée
Est le don de prudence heureusement entée.
Au cerveau de ce Maire: ô que sil estoit creu
Iamais Ils ne seroient consumés par le feu.

Le maire
Adieu & vous gardez de vous livrer en proye
Pour dire mais trop tard helas je n'y pensoye

Le Syndique
"Il faut par tous moyens plustost que par effort
"Faire que l'ennemy cognoisse qu'il a tort
Appellez donc Poulin. Ca venez capitaine
Dites nous sil vous plaist la cause qui vous meine

Poulin
La cause vrais Chrestiens vostre bien seulement
Et à fin qu'asseurez n'en doubtiez nullement
Premierement le Dieu que vous priez j'invoque
Qu'il vueille presider sur ce present colloque
Qu'il n'y soit dit ne fait rien contre son honneur
Rien contre vous enfans du Toutpuissant Seigneur
Ce fondement bien mis au nom de vostre Pere
Tel que vous me voyez tenez moy vostre frere
D'autant que du profond gouffre d'iniquité

*Tragedy of the Sack of Cabrières*　　　　　　　　　　　　　　　99

[9v]

Yet he who wishes to see the curring blade, once arms,[1]
Restored to his plowshare must avoid this sedition.
Mayor, withdraw, to prevent such a disaster.

The Mayor
This is wise counsel, for the death of Christians is no tragedy.

The Chorus
Celestial fire, stolen, some pretend, by Prometheus,[2]
Is the gift of prudence luckily grafted
To the mind of this mayor. O! Had he been believed,
Never would they have been consumed by fire!

The Mayor
Farewell, and do not surrender yourselves
Like prey, so that you will not say, alas too late, "I did not foresee it!"

The Syndic
"We must, by any means, but not by force,
"Push the enemy to admit his error.
Call forth Poulin. Come here, captain,
Please tell us the reason why you came hither.

Poulin
The sole reason why I came, O true Christians, is your own sake!
And, first of all, so that reassured, you might not doubt my reason,
I invoke the God to whom you pray.
May he preside over our assembly,
So that nothing may be uttered or done against his honor,
Or against you, children of the almighty God.
Once this foundation is well established, in the name of your father,
Please receive me here as your brother,
Especially since, from the depth of iniquity

---

[1] It is not the plow itself that is the weapon here, but instead the share, its metallic blade-like part that digs into the soil to trace furrows. It could also be used by the author as an analogy for the vouge, a thirteenth-century spear, the blade of which looked like a share. Also, a potential reference to Joel 3:10: "Beat your plowshares into swords / And your pruning hooks into spears; / Let the weak say, 'I am strong.'"

[2] Prometheus, the titan who created mankind and who stole fire from Zeus to give it to man. A clear symbol of wisdom, the author underlines here the lack of discernment of the Vaudois, whose overconfidence and trust in a peaceful solution brought them to their demise. Ironically, fire, instead of saving them, will be their end, in a reversal of fate.

[10r]

Mon Dieu m'a fait surgir au port de vérité　　　　　　　　　10
Pour le glorifier je n'ay honte de dire
Meschant! que i'ay osé de ma mère mesdire
Comme d'une putain pour estre par tel art
Du seigneur de Grignan reputé le bastard
Plus tost que d'estre au vray dit le fils legitime
De mon pere un pouvre hoste homme de nulle estime
Vray est qu'entre les Turcs j'ay apris à mentir
Mais pleurant je ne fay las que m'en repentir
Christ ne m'a pas instruit en sa vérité sainte
Qu'il ne m'ait fait hayr toute parolle feinte
Bien que tousiours Poulin bastard on jurera
Poulin pourtant menteur trouvé plus ne sera
Vostre tant bon seigneur est poulsé d'un tel zele
Qu'il m'a rendu en Christ la grace à Dieu fidele
Ce qu'estre je ne puis sans vous delivrer tous
Ou bien que je ne meure aujourd'huy avec vous

Le Syndique
Le Sieur de Catderousse & sieur de ceste ville
Pourrroit il bien entendre & aimer l'Evangile

Poulin
Pour vous en asseurer d'un grand cœur il m'a dit
Que plustost que souffrir à cest homme maudit
Toucher du bout du doigt une seule personne
À mille morts pour vous sa vie il abandonne
De moy voicy le point sachez que quand Je voy
Si constante envers Dieu et envers vous sa foy
Cij

*Tragedy of the Sack of Cabrières*   101

[10r]

My God made me anchor at the harbor of truth
To glorify him. I am not afraid to say,
"Oh, I am a villain!," I who did dare to slander my own mother,
And name her a whore, so as to be by this ruse
Considered the bastard of the Lord of Grignan,
Instead of being the son of my legitimate father,
His poor subject, worthy of no interest.
It is true that among the Turks, I learned how to lie;
But crying, all I do, alas, is repent.
Christ has not elevated me in his holy truth
So that I might hate all the false words.
Even though they will always swear Poulin is a bastard,
Poulin the liar will nevermore be found.[1]
Your good Lord is so zealous,
That he made me faithful, God be thanked.
I cannot be faithful if I do not save you all,
Or die today with you.

The Syndic
Could the Lord of Catderousse, sire of this town,
Also hear and love the Gospels?

Poulin
To reassure you, he affirmed with all his heart
That instead of suffering[2] that this evil man
Dare to lay a single finger on any of you,
To a thousand deaths he would give up his life.
Here is my point; know that when I see
His faith so constant toward you and God,

---

[1] Because of his new commitment to Christ, the lies will no longer flow out of Poulin's mouth, even though his previous errors (here, his lack of response to who his true father was) are still impacting his current life. See Matt. 12:36: "But I say to you that for every idle word men may speak, they will give account of it in the day of judgment."

[2] The original expression of "souffrir que," besides the idea of "bearing, accepting," also plays in the whole plot of Catderousse and d'Opède.

[10v]

Je luy baise la main & hautement m'escrie
Mourons pour eux ou bien sauvons les je vous prie
Il respond qu'il est prest demande seulement
Que je luy vueille ouvrir le moyen & comment
Il faut que nous allons (luy di je) expres defendre
À ce sot president de rien plus entreprendre
Sur nul de vos subiects ne sur leur bien aussi
Que dans demain il vuide & tout ce camp d'icy
Autrement il scaura qu'un Gentilhomme en guerre
Des mains d'un Advocat scait bien garder sa terre
Quant est du different pour vostre foy esmeu
Qu'il en soit par le Roy chrestiennement cogneu
Le tout ainsi conclu nous allons à D'Opede
Luy d'un front refrongné d'une grimace laide
Et d'un regard hideux nous cuide espouventer
Vous l'eussiez veu crier se battre & tourmenter
Et qui pis est vomir blasphemes execrables
Mais nonobstant ses cris si fermes & si stables
Persister il nous veoit ou qu'il luy faut mourir
Ou à son barreau d'Aix vistement recourir
Car j'avoy pratiqué souldars & capitaines
Qui contre luy jestoient la rage de leurs haines
Criant que ce larron ce vieil asne cassé
Tout à cest'heure soit par les piques passé

*Tragedy of the Sack of Cabrières*
103

[10v]

I kiss his hand,[1] and loudly proclaim,
"Let us either die for them, or save them, I beg you!"
He replied to me that he was ready to do so, and simply asks
That I give him a means to his end.
We have to go, I told him, convince
This foolish president not to take any further actions
Against any of your subjects, or their possessions.
We must ask him to break camp and leave tomorrow,
Otherwise he will discover that a gentleman in war
Knows how to keep his land out of the hands of a lawyer.
Concerning the disagreement raised concerning your faith,
May the king be made aware of it in a Christian manner.[2]
Once this is decided, let us go see d'Opède,
He who, with his sullen forehead, his ugly grin,
And his hideous stare thinks he frightens us.
If only you had seen him shout, fight, and torment,
And, worse than anything, spit out execrable blasphemy![3]
Notwithstanding his firm and continuous screams,
We shall persist; either he will die,
Or he will have to resort to the court at Aix.[4]
I have won over soldiers and officers[5]
Who hurled the rage of their hatred against him,
Claiming that this thief, this old worn ass,
Should be immediately stabbed to death by pikes.

---

[1] The use of the French term "baisemain" shows the exaggerated reaction to the actions of Catderousse, obscuring once again either Poulin's credulity in his conversion, or on the contrary his participation in the plot to take down Cabrières.

[2] These lines once again put the play in its historical context, while at the same time pushing forward the fact that Francis I knew about the Waldensians, thus reinforcing his responsibility in the massacre to come.

[3] This whole part is also to be put in dialogue with the conversion of Poulin. The author deliberately blurs the vision of its reader or its audience by not making clear whether Poulin is already changed or if his declarations are part of a vile plan to destroy the Waldensians. Here, the accusations of villainy are intermingled with his own hypocrisy, if he is faking his ideas, or his repentance.

[4] D'Opède, as the president of the parliament, is nevertheless subjected to the law, hence this nod to the bar.

[5] My translation of "capitaines" as "officers" is here designed to show how, in Poulin's discourse, both the simple soldiers and their leaders consider that d'Opède is a terrible president, not worthy of being respected.

Luy (comme des deux maux on doit prendre le moindre
À l'accord de vuider contraint est venu joindre
"Car l'homme qui ne peut faire ainsi comm'Il veut
"Contrait est de vouloir seulement ce qu'il peut

He, because of two evils one must take the lesser,
Finally accepted to leave, constrained to do so.
"For the man who cannot do whatever he pleases,
"Is forced to do whatever he may.[1]

---

[1] Even though this looks like a proverb, it is not found in any catalogs of proverbs. However, this looks like a direct reference to Terence, which is quoted by Augustine in book 14, chapter 25 of *City of God:* "Come then, let us behold him living as he wishes, since he has put the screw on himself and ordered himself not to wish for what is beyond his power, but to wish for what he can get; in the words of Terence, 'Since what you wish is not what is within your power / Direct your wish to what you can achieve.'" The original quotation comes from *Andria*, act 2, sc. 1: "Quoniam non potest id fieri quod vis, id velis quod possit." See Augustine, *City of God,* ed. David Knowles (New York: Penguin Books, 1972), 590.

[11r]

Le Syndique 11
Quel accord s'il vous plaist dites le en sa substance

Poulin
C'est que pour sa descharge & pour son asseurance
Sans laisser un seul point vous mettrez par escrit
La foy que vous avez au Pere en Jesuchrist
Au saint Esprit aussi; qu'à d'Opede à ceste heure
Le tout clos soit porté à fin qu'il ne demeure
Pour quatre mille escus c'est sa derniere main
Vostre seigneur pour vous s'est monstré si humain
Qu'il a promis payer la somme toute entiere
Regardez regardez fideles de Cabriere
Comme le Dieu vivant vostre unique secours
Vous retire au jourd'huy des pattes de cest ours
À fin qu'ici tousiours vous chantiez les louanges
De Dieu qui seul a fait merveilles si estranges
En delivrant les siens qu'il rend leurs ennemys
Par son esprit changez en leurs plus grands amis
Ainsi changé par luy autheur de ma venue
Ie ne cerche sinon que ma foy soit cognue
Entre vous par les fruits de Sainte Charité
Tesmoignage certain de ma fidelité
Maintenant c'est à vous de veoir sur cest affaire
Et si je puis encor quelqu'autre chose faire
Vous ne m'espargnerez, l'effet vous fera veoir,
Que j'auray comm'amy fait du tout mon devoir
Pour la fin Je vous pri de faire en telle sorte
Que ce vilain s'en aille tenir ailleurs escorte

Le Syndique
Ciij

[11r]

The Syndic
What agreement? Tell us in substance, please.

Poulin
It is that, for his respite and his safety,
You shall, without leaving out a single point, write down
The elements of your faith in the Father and Jesus Christ,
And in the Holy Spirit;[1] they will then be brought to d'Opède,
Securely sealed, in order for him to not remain here;
You will also give him four thousand ecus; it is his last offer.[2]
Your lord was so humane that he proposed
To pay for you the whole sum.
Look, look, oh faithful people of Cabrières,
How the living God, your sole comfort,
Is saving you today from the claws of this bear,
So that here you can ever sing the praise
Of God, who alone works such wonderful mysteries,
By delivering his people; he turns their enemies
By the strength of his spirit into their greatest friends.
Thus I was changed by him, and he made me come here.
I do not seek anything, but for my faith to be known
Among you, by the fruits of his holy Charity,
A firm testimony of my fidelity;
Now, it is up to you to judge me on this matter.
And if I may still be of any help,
Please do not spare me; thus you will realize
That, like a friend, I did my entire duty.
Finally, I beg you to do everything you can
To send this villainous man and his troop further away.

The Syndic

---

[1] We should see this demand by d'Opède as the final sign of his treachery: by asking the Waldensians to write down the basis of their faith, he de facto asks them to write what is considered as heresy, thus providing evidence that the upcoming massacre was justified to rid the kingdom of those who were not adhering to the national faith.

[2] This sum, based on the data of the money converter website "Convertisseur de monnaie d'ancien régime" (http://convertisseur-monnaie-ancienne.fr), would represent almost 632,700 Euros, or US$713,000 as of June 15, 2020. The act of asking for money could also be seen as a reference to Judas Iscariot, who sold Christ, as stated in Matt. 27:9: "And they took the thirty pieces of silver, the value of Him who was priced, whom they of the children of Israel priced." The Waldensians, following the traditional reformist trope of themselves as the people of God, are then sold to their martyrdom for a sum of money.

[11v]

Si là avec le Maire il vous plaist deviser
Nous pourrons entre nous plus libres adviser
Ou si nous vous devons à poursuyvre semondre
Et vous remercier ou autrement respondre

Poulin

Je m'en vay avec luy faites tout à loysir
Et vous gardez du mal en lieu du bien choisir

Le Maire & Poulin

Le Maire, Poulin

Voici venir Poulin Poulin nostre ruine

Poulin

Contre ce fin rusé faut que je contremine

Le maire

Mon Dieu tu me retiens qu'à ce traistre menteur
Ie ne donne du plomb droitement dans le cœur
Ô maudite harquebuse ô maudites plombées
Tant de personnes sont mortes par vous tombées.
Hélas! estoit ce à fin maintenant d'espargner
Ce meschant pour le faire en nostre sang baigner
Ah! que n'est il permis de bien faire en tuant
Et le sang estancher du sang d'un sanguinaire
Que tu n'y serves rien malheureux pistolet!

*Tragedy of the Sack of Cabrières*　　　　　　　　　　　　　　　　　109

[11v]

If it pleases you to talk to the Mayor,
We shall more easily debate among ourselves
Whether we need to convoke you
And thank you or respond otherwise.

Poulin
I leave with him; do as you wish,
But be sure to choose good, and not evil.

The Mayor and Poulin

The Mayor
Here comes Poulin, Poulin our ruin.

Poulin
I have to undermine this cunning man.[1]

The Mayor
Dear God, you are keeping me from attacking this wretched liar,
And from piercing his heart with a volley of shots!
O damned arquebus, O cursed bullets!
So many people died, felled by you!
Alas! Did this happen to now spare
This villain, so that he can bathe in our own blood?[2]
Ah! How is it forbidden to do good in killing,
And staunch all that splattered blood with the blood of a bloody assassin?
Why are you of no use, miserable pistol?

---

[1] The word "contremine" designates an underground tunnel designed to protect itself from the bombing of an assailant, close to the modern idea of trench. I decided here to translate the expression in a way that transcribes how Poulin is aware that trumping the Mayor will be much harder than fooling the Syndic.

[2] Boccassini sees in this tirade a reference to Pierre de Ronsard's "Les Armes. A Jean Brinon" (1555). The allusion to death and violence are the same, and particularly the idea of good men dying in the place of bad ones, and evil people not suffering the lot they deserve. Ronsard explains indeed: "car les hommes plus forts / Sont aujourd'huy tuez d'un poltron en cachette / A coups de harquebouze, ou a coup de mousquette" (and the strongest of men / Are nowadays killed by a hidden coward / Who shot them with his arquebus or with a musket). See Pierre de Ronsard, *Œuvres complètes*, ed. Gustave Cohen (Paris: Gallimard, 1950), 2:313.

Rien malheureux Canon! rien malheureux boulet!
Ô malheureux salpestre, ô malheureuse poudre
Puis que ce traistre à Dieu vous ne bruslez en foudre

Poulin

Garde qu'à cestui ci tu ne sois descouvert
Poulin ou tu seras percé à jour ouvert

*Tragedy of the Sack of Cabrières*                                                    111

Of no use, O miserable cannon? Of no use, O miserable cannonball?
O miserable saltpeter,[1] O miserable gunpowder,
Since you will not blast this traitor to God!

Poulin
Be wary not to be discovered by this fellow,
Poulin, or you will be stabbed in broad daylight.

---

[1] Saltpeter (from Medieval Latin *salpetrae,* literally "ground salt") is a chemical component known since at least before the Middle Ages and used in gunpowder and explosives. Its chemical name is potassium nitrate.

[12r]

Mon frère voyez vous ces sept qui se pourmeinent
Et couplez deux à deux grand suite apres eux meinent

Le Maire

Si ie les voy? Oui il y a ia long temps

Poulin

Ô qu'ils sont de me veoir en ce lieu malcontens!
Car ils n'ignorent pas qu'à chacun ie racompte
Leurs vies qui feroyent Sathan rougir de honte
Ce monstre qui la rage escume furieux
Ce premier di ie à qui le feu sort par les yeux
Ce visage emprunté ceste teste pointue
Ce gros groin de pourceau cest aller de tortue
Ces grands oreilles d'asne & ces grands dens de loup
Ce col à vis froncé dans le corps tout à coup
Ces levres contre Dieu à blasphémer hardies
Ces doigts crochez ainçois ces gryphes de Harpyes
Qui contaminent tout ce qui est touché
Ces aixelles fy fy ou le bouc est caché
Ce grand gouffre de ventre estayé sur deux piles
Legières à destruire autrement immobiles
Dont le fondement est de deux pieds de gryphon
Ceste beste puante & de faict & de nom
Puante si puant avant qu'elle soit morte
Que d'un mill'la sentant la femme grosse avorte
C'est d'Opede Minier ah le ladre pourri
Par les Tygres petit fut de leur sang nourry
Depuis ses premieres ans ces premiers mets de Thrace
Jusqu'a crever l'on fait ainsi sanglante masse
D'un corps si bien marqué iugez quel est l'esprit
Qui fors que cruauté rien en son temps n'apprit

Ciiij

*Tragedy of the Sack of Cabrières*

[12r]

Dear brother, can you see these seven men who are marching all over,
With their great entourage following, two by two?[1]

The Mayor
Can I see them? Yes, and I have for a long time.

Poulin
O! How displeased they are to see me here!
For they well know that I will tell everyone
About their lives, which would make Satan himself blush from shame.
This furious monster, rabid and foaming,
This first one, with fire darting from his eyes,
This deceitful face, this pointy head,
This fat swine snout, this gait of a tortoise,
These long ass ears, and these wolf fangs,
This face fastened directly to the body,
These lips emboldened to blaspheme against God,
These crooked fingers, like the claws of harpies,
Besmirching all the things that they touch,
These armpits, fie! fie!, where the billy goat is hiding,
This great, abysmal gut, propped up on two pillars
Easy to destroy, otherwise immobile,
For which the bottom are two griffin feet,
This noxious beast, in name and actions,
So foul and stinking, even before it died,
That, smelling it from a mile away, the woman big with child has a miscarriage:
This man is d'Opède Meynier.[2] Ah, what a rotten leper!
When he was a baby, tigers fed him with their own blood;
From his very first years, these Thracian[3] foods
Turned him into such a bloody mass that he nearly burst.
With such a distorted body, guess what his mind is like,
For it was never taught anything save for cruelty.

The third one, with his swarthy skin, shows us clearly from his looks

---

[1] A reference to *The Seven against Thebes* by Aeschylus.

[2] "Meynier" was the first part of d'Opède's family name.

[3] Thracians were perceived as a violent people. See Henrik Berg, "Masculinities in Early Hellenistic Athens," in *What Is Masculinity? Historical Dynamics from Antiquity to the Contemporary World*, ed. J. Arnold and S. Brady (Basingstoke: Palgrave-MacMillan, 2013), 97–113.

[12v]

Tel le corps tel l'esprit homme ne scauroit dire
Lequel des deux le plus son compaignon empire
Ce monstre si hideux ores dans son chasteau
Bat la fausse monnoye or'y tient le bourdeau
Ouvert à tous venans là cest inceste infame
Fait de sa propre seur sa legitime femme
Et pour mieux se monstrer le meschant des meschans
Il a fait là le sang regorger par les champs

Le maire
Mais qui est cestuy là qui l'accoste & le touche
Et comm'un gros matin tourne vire & se couche?

Poulin
C'est son vilain de genre en toute cruauté
Pire que son beau pere & en desloyauté
Pour scavoir ses vertus contentez vous en somme
Que iamais le Soleil ne veid si meschant homme

Le maire
Ces deux qu'on voit apres si braves se marcher?

Poulin
Ô qu'ils voudroyent vous veoir tous en pieces hascher!
Le plus petit des deux à fait mourir son frere
L'autre a rendu la mort pour sa vie à sa mere

Le maire
Et cest autre fuyant sçavez vous qui il est?

Poulin
Ie ne le scay que trop dont fort il m'en desplaist
Il n'est Sathan ny homme ains pire que le diable
Car la divinité il dist n'estre que fable

*Tragedy of the Sack of Cabrières*                                                   115

[12v]

Like body like spirit: no one could tell
Which of the two corrupts the other more.
This hideous monster, hidden in his castle,
Mints counterfeit money,[1] and maintains a brothel
Opened for all to come. In there, this infamous, incestuous fiend
Takes his sister for his legitimate wife.
And to prove that he is the most evil of all evil men,
He floods the fields with blood.

The Mayor
But who is he, who approaches and brushes against him,
And like a mastiff [2] turns around him, and then sits down?

Poulin
It is his villainous son-in-law, in all cruelty
And disloyalty worse than his father-in-law.
To be acquainted with his virtues, you simply have to know
That never has the sun seen such an evil man.

The Mayor
And those two, who are so boldly walking together?

Poulin
O! How they wish they could see you hacked to pieces!
The smaller of the two killed his own brother;
The other one repaid with death his mother who gave him life.

The Mayor
And this fellow who is fleeing, do you know who he is?

Poulin
I know him too well, and this displeases me greatly.
Neither Satan nor any man is worse than this devil,
For he says that divinity is just fable.

---

[1] The notion of counterfeit money has a double meaning. It is obviously a forbidden activity, but can also be seen from the symbolic point of view as the idea of counterfeiting purity (gold, precious metals) for one's benefit, thus emphasizing the evil of the process.
[2] "Matin" refers to the Neapolitan mastiff, a very ancient breed that was known for its massive size.

Des autres le premier n'a point aussi de Dieu
Non plus que le second qui se marche au milieu

Le maire
Le tiers tant basanné monstre bien à sa mine

*Tragedy of the Sack of Cabrières*

Of the others, the first has no belief in God,
Nor does the second one, he who walks in the middle.

The Mayor
The third one, with his swarthy skin, shows us clearly from his looks

[13r]

Que pour estre bourreau homme n'y a plus digne          13

Poulin
Croyez qu'on ne pourroit iamais depeindre au vif
Les vices malheureux de ce malheureux Juif

Le maire
Monsieur de Catderousse ou est il à cest heure?

Poulin
S'il est veu avec eux prenez moy que je meure
Car il les a en haine & tant que soufflera
Du Pole Articq' la bise il ne les aimera

Le maire
Allons on nous rappelle ô combien je voudroye
Que ce cheval ne feist de Cabriere une Troye

Le Syndique Poulin & le Maire

Le Syndique
Nous remercions Dieu de ce qu'il a usé
De sa grace envers vous paravant abusé
Aux erreurs de Sathan en vous monstrant sa voye
Voye que qui la suit garde n'a qu'il fourvoyé
Graces nous luy rendons de vostre volonté
Pour nous heuresement remettre en liberté
Aumoins s'il est ainsi que vous venez de dire.

*Tragedy of the Sack of Cabrières*

[13r]

That nobody is more suitable than he is to be an executioner.

Poulin
Do you think it will ever be possible to truly depict
All the ruinous vices of this wretched Jew?[1]

The Mayor
Where is the lord of Catderousse at this moment?

Poulin
If he is seen with them, strike me down, so I can die.
For he hates them, and for as long as blows the wind
From the Arctic, he shall not love them.

The Mayor
Let us go, we are summoned. O, how I wish
That this horse would not turn Cabrières into a new Troy![2]

The Syndic, Poulin, and the Mayor

The Syndic
We are grateful to God, for he granted his grace
To you, who were deceived before
By the guile of Satan, and he showed you his way,
In which he keeps whoever follows it from being led astray.
We are grateful to him for your decision
To free us, and bring happiness upon us,
At least if this happens as you just explained.

---

[1] Traditional anti-Semitic trope, still very much present in the sixteenth century. Jews were seen as evil persons. Comparing d'Opède to one shows the extent of the disgust that Poulin wants to convey.

[2] The Trojan horse, used by the Greek troops to enter into Troy and finally subdue the city, as seen in Virgil's *Aeneid*, book 2: "The Greeks grew weary of the tedious war, / And by Minerva's aid a fabric rear'd, / Which like a steed of monstrous height appear'd: / The sides were plank'd with pine; they feign'd it made / For their return, and this the vow they paid. / Thus they pretend, but in the hollow side / Selected numbers of their soldiers hide: / With inward arms the dire machine they load, / And iron bowels stuff the dark abode." (trans. John Dryden, Internet Classics Archive, http://classics.mit.edu/Virgil/aeneid.2.ii.html). The Trojan horse here is also a pun on Poulin's name (a "poulain" is a colt), underlining the fact that the Mayor fears he might himself be bringing doom upon his people by letting Poulin in.

### Poulin
Ah faites moy mourir c'est ce que je desire
Ie suis las de tant vivre ô mort mon seul repos
Puis que ces gens de bien doubtent de mes propos

### Le Syndique
La plus part les croit bien mais jamais n'est si ferme
Ce qu'on dit simplement comme ce qu'on afferme      Dj

### Poulin

*Tragedy of the Sack of Cabrières* 121

Poulin
Ah, make me die! That is what I desire.
I am weary of living, O death, my only respite,
Since these good people doubt my promises.

The Syndic
Most do believe them, but nothing that is said is more assured
Than that which is assured under oath.

Poulin

[13v]

Ô souverain seigneur qui tient tout sous ta main
Seigneur qui nous defens de ton nom prendre en vain
Et qui as condamné avecques le periure
Celuy qui en mespris pour neant ton nom jure
Ô Seigneur qui destruis les traistres & menteurs
Et vois plus profond de l'abysme des cœurs
Je te prie Eternel que sur moy tu desserres
Tes foudres tes esclairs, tes esclattans tonnerres
Qu'à présent J'en soy'ars de tout salut forclos
Si pour ce peuple saint que ce camp tient enclos
Ie n'ay pris le combat & trouvé la maniere
Pour sauver auiourd'huy & delivrer Cabriere
Que ie soye ô mon Dieu comme Cain maudit
S'il n'est ainsi du tout comme je leur ay dit
Et qu'éternellement de ton fils le merite
En lieu de t'appaiser plus contre moy s'irrite
Le Ciel me soit fermé la fureur de la mer
Me vienne au plus hideux des gouffres abismer
L'air pour m'entretenir de tous venins m'emplisse
La terre ne me porte encor moins me nourisse
Si du tout je n'ay dit la pure vérité
N'ayes jamais Seigneur de ce Poulin pitié

Le Syndique
A ceste heure on vous croit toutesfois je puis dire
Que mieux on vous eust creu sans ainsi vous maudire

Poulin
Pour affermer le vray est ce fait meschamment
D'en faire juge Dieu qui seul scait si on ment?

Le maire
Je crains que vray ne soit en ce vilain qui jure

# Tragedy of the Sack of Cabrières

[13v]

O sovereign Lord, who holds everything in your hand!
Lord, who forbids us from taking your name in vain,
And who condemned for perjury
Those who scornfully swore in your name for nothing!
O Lord, who destroys the traitors and liars
And who sees deep in the abyss of our hearts
I beg you, Eternal Father, to unleash on me
Your lightning and your thunderbolts, your exploding thunderstorm.
May they now burn me, excluded from salvation,
If, for this holy people, trapped in this encampment,
I have not taken arms and found a way
Today to save and deliver Cabrières.
May I be, O my God, cursed like Cain,[1]
If things do not happen just as I told them.
And may the merit of your son eternally
Anger you against me, instead of appeasing me.
May the heavens be closed to me; may furious waves
Drag me away into the most hideous of depths;
May the air that sustains me fill me with venom;
May the earth not bear me, and much less feed me,
If all I told was not pure truth,
Please, Lord, never have pity for this Poulin!

The Syndic
We believe you for now. Nevertheless, I can say
That we would have trusted you better, if you had not cursed yourself.

Poulin
Is it being a villain to swear things are true,
And to choose God for a judge, who alone knows if we lie?

The Mayor
I fear there is nothing to trust in this villain who swears.

---

[1] The murder of Abel by Cain. Because he was angry that his brother's offering had pleased God more than his own, Cain killed him: "Now Cain talked with Abel his brother; and it came to pass, when they were in the field, that Cain rose up against Abel his brother and killed him'"" (Gen. 4:8). He thus became the first murderer in biblical time.

[14r]

Que plus jure vilain plus vilain se pariure 14

Le Syndique
Nous accordons le tout voicy de nostre part
Les points de nostre foy icy escrits à part
Scellez & cachetez nostre foy sera veue
Par là telle qu'elle est tousiours par nous tenue
Le Maire & moy l'irons au nom de tous porter
Et à qui vous voudrez hardiment presenter

Le Maire
À la charge Messieurs qu'y laisserons la vie
C'est honneur que pour Christ elle nous soit ravie

Poulin
Dieu vous face en sa foy heureux vivre & mourir
Au reste il faut encor pour mieux vous secourir
Que Catderousse ou moy expressement à l'heure
Qu'on levera le siege en la ville demeure
A la routte d'un camp tousiours y a danger
Que les souldars cassez ne courent saccager
Si tost qu'on sonnera. Serre serre bagage
Vous nous aurez tous deux et quelqu'autre en hostage

Le Syndique
Nous nous fions en vous croyez que nous ferons
Ce que nous conseillez & qu'ingrats ne serons
Ny envers vous monsieur ny envers nostre maistre

Le maire
Ô mon Dieu s'obliger à bien faire à un traistre

Poulin
Ca mes deux freres ca allons & qu'on ne cede
Rien de l'honneur de Dieu à ce meschant d'Opede

Le maire
Jesuchrist m'a donné une si vive foy
Que je confesseray l'honneur que je luy doy     Dij

[14r]

The more this villain swears, the more villainously he forswears.

The Syndic
We acknowledge all these points. Here for our part are
The articles of our faith written one by one,
Sealed and marked. Our faith will be seen
In this as it has always been held by us.
The Mayor and I will go carry it, in the name of all of us,
To whomever you will boldly introduce to us.

The Mayor
It is our duty, gentlemen who will die from it!
It is an honor that we would die for Christ.

Poulin
God grant you to live and die happily in his faith.
Besides, in order to protect you, it is necessary
That either Catderousse or I, at the time
That the siege is lifted, stay here in the city.
On the path out of a camp, there is always danger
That angry soldiers would come and pillage.
As soon as we ring the bells, "Take, take your belongings,"
You will hold the two of us and a few others hostage.

The Syndic
We put our trust in you, be assured that we will do
As you are advising us to, and that we shall not be ungrateful
Neither against you, nor against our master.

The Mayor
O my God! To be compelled to be civil to a traitor!

Poulin
There, my two brothers, there! Let us go, and let us not cede
Any of God's honor to this evil d'Opède.

The Mayor
Jesus Christ granted me such a living faith
That I will confess the honor that I owe him.

[14v]

Le Syndique
Il n'y à glaive ou feu qui m'empesche de dire
Qu'il est mon seul Sauveur ne m'en face desdire

LE CHŒUR

La langue maudite
En sucre & en miel
Mesle et rend confite
Sa poison de fiel
Poison nonpareille
Quy tant seulement
En touchant l'oreille
Tue ne un moment.

Elle n'a point d'ailes
Et volle en tous lieux
Ses flesches mortelles
Darde jusqu'aux cieux
De la mort la source
Source de tout mal
N'a roulé sa course
Par autre canal.

Nostre premier pere
Par elle deceu
Oyant la vipere
Peche a conceu

*Tragedy of the Sack of Cabrières*  127

[14v]

The Syndic
Neither sword nor fire will prevent me from saying
That he is my sole savior, and this do not make me deny.

The Chorus

The cursed tongue
Mixes its venomous bile
In sugar and in sweet honey,
And preserves it,
An unrivaled poison
That simply,
By touching the ear,
Immediately kills.[1]

Speech has no wings,
Yet it can fly everywhere;
Its deadly arrows
Can reach the heavens.
The source of death
And source of all evils
Takes its course
Through no other channel.

Our prime father,
Deceived by it,
When he listened to the serpent,
Conceived sin.[2]

---

[1] Just like the previous monologue, the Chorus is making a demonstration of the dangerous power of evil words, and how they can destroy and cause more damage than actual physical violence, because speech can destroy the immortal soul.

[2] The first father is Adam, and this excerpt is a reference to the original sin, in Gen. 3:1: "Now the serpent was more cunning than any beast of the field which the LORD God had made." We note here a change from the original story of the Bible, in which it is, in Gen. 3:4–6, Eve who is tempted and who succumbs first to the serpent: "Then the serpent said to the woman, 'You will not surely die./ For God knows that in the day you eat of it your eyes will be opened, and you will be like God, knowing good and evil.'/ So when the woman saw that the tree was good for food, that it was pleasant to the eyes, and a tree desirable to make one wise, she took of its fruit and ate."

Peche dont le gage
L'eternelle mort
Tout l'humain lignage
Lotit sous son sort.

*Tragedy of the Sack of Cabrières*

Sin whose consequence,
Eternal death,
Plagues the whole human lineage
With its poor fate.

[15r]

Et quand la traistresse                                          15
Adam a perdu
La terre elle engresse
Du sang espandu
Par le parricide
Quy en taint ses mains
Quand le monde il vuide
Du quart des humain

Toutes phrenesies
Toute faulseté
Toutes heresies,
Toute impiete
La langue fait croire
Pour la verité
Et le Dieu de gloire
Estre vanité.

Ce que langue on nomme
Ce feut le docteur
Qui feit que Sodome
Abysma d'horreur
Elle est la sereine
Qui doux en chantant
Dans le gouffre meine
Quiconque l'entend

Les Juifs tant affole
Que de leur thresor                         Diij

*Tragedy of the Sack of Cabrières* 131

[15r]

And when this treacherous speech
Caused the ruin of Adam,
It enriched the soil
With the blood it did shed
Through parricide,
It tainted his hands
When it emptied the world
Of a quarter of the humans.[1]

All frenzy,
All duplicity,
All heresies,
All impiety,
That is what the tongue makes us believe
To be true,
And accuses you, the God of glory,
To be nothing.

What we name words,
Were the pedants[2]
Who caused Sodom[3]
To be destroyed by horror.
They are the sirens
Who, with their sweet songs,
Drag to the chasm
Whoever listens to them.

It made the Jews so insane
That with their treasure

---

[1] There were, according to the Bible, only four humans then (Adam and Eve, Abel, and Cain); Cain then indeed killed a quarter of humanity, just like the Chorus explains.

[2] In this specific context, I translated "docteur" through the word "docte," meaning "well-learned" but also "pedantic," which corresponds to the general meaning depicted here.

[3] Sodom and Gomorrah, the two biblical cities that were destroyed by God because of their lewd behavior. Two angels were sent by God to "investigate" the situation there; they were hosted by Lot, Abraham's nephew. When the men of the city ("both old and young") heard about their arrival, they asked Lot to "bring them out to us so that we may know them carnally" (Gen. 19:4–5).

[15v]

Fondans une idole
Dressent le veau d'or
Luy font sacrifice
Sans aucun remord
Joyeux en leur vice
Y dansent d'accord

Et à Samarie
Fausse promet l'heur
De veoir de Syrie
Son prince vainqueur
Qui d'une sagette
Tout outre persé
Cheut de sa charrette
Mourant renversé

D'une eau fort petite
L'honneur du torrent
Commençant sa fuite
Si roide la rend
Que les rocs il roule
Tirez de leur fort
Ainsi qu'une boule
Partant d'un bras fort

*Tragedy of the Sack of Cabrières*

[15v]

That they melt, they build an idol
That they erect as the golden calf.[1]
They offer him sacrifices,
With no remorse,
Joyous in their vice,
And dancing with joy.

And to Samaria,
False, it promises the happiness
Of witnessing, from Syria,
Its victorious prince
Who, by an arrow,
Was pierced through;
He falls down from his chariot,
And dies.[2]

From trickling water,
The force of the torrent,
Beginning its course,
Makes the river so strong,
That it rolls boulders
From their fortress
Just like a ball
Thrown by a strong arm.

---

[1] The golden calf that the people of Israel built and started adoring during Moses's absence on Mount Sinai (Exod. 32:4: "And he received the gold from their hand, and he fashioned it with an engraving tool, and made a molded calf. Then they said, 'This is your god, O Israel, that brought you out of the land of Egypt!'"). This stanza and the one that immediately follows are written in the present tense, showing that these events are seen as a commentary for the present situation.

[2] See 1 Kings 22:34: "Now a certain man drew a bow at random, and struck the king of Israel between the joints of his armor. So he said to the driver of his chariot, 'Turn around and take me out of the battle, for I am wounded.'"

Ainsi d'une mouche
La langue nous rend
Tant soit peu la touche
Un grand Elephant
D'elle vint la rage
Pourquoy ce grand tout

*Tragedy of the Sack of Cabrières*  135

Speech changes us,
With the slightest touch,
From a fly
Into a great elephant.[1]
Rage comes from them,
Which is also why this great world,

---

[1] The French proverb "Faire d'une mouche un éléphant" (literally "turn a fly into an elephant") could be translated into the English idiom "to make a mountain out of a molehill." It is used here to condemn how slander can mislead people.

[16r]

Noyé par naufrage
Fut de l'eau en bout                                      16

Et sa fin soudaine
Viendra par le feu
Que ceste vilaine
Soufle peu à peu
Comme d'une amorce
On veoit ondoyer
La flamme qu'a force
On ne ne peut noyer

Elle calomnie
Tousiours verité
Et tousiours denie,
La droite equite
Par elle le vice
Est nomme vertu
Et droit & justice
Ce qui est tortu.

Mais qui rompt les treves
Couvans trahison
Ou qui fait les vefves
N'est ce toy tison
Qui langue te nommes
Langue qui du flanc
Des plus divins hommes
Fais courir le sang                      Diiij

*Tragedy of the Sack of Cabrières*

[16r]

Drowned by the shipwreck,
Was devoured by water.

And its sudden death
Will come from the fire
Blown little by little
By this ugly speech:
Just like the fuse,
On which dances
The flame that, even with force,
Cannot be extinguished.

The tongue slanders
The truth, always,
And always rejects
Rightful equity.
Through its action, vice
Becomes virtue,
And law and justice
Are wronged.

Who breaks the truces,
Hatches treason,
Or turns women into widows?
Would it not be you, firebrand
Named tongue,
Tongue that, from the side
Of the holiest of men,
Sheds blood?[1]

---

[1] The humanity of Christ, who was injured and bled when he was pierced with a spear.

[16v]

Langue veneneuse
Au mary sa foy
La plus vertueuse
Viole par toy
La vierge pudique
Tu livres en main
Au paillard lubrique
Lubrique putain

Qui perd la jenesse?
Tes allechemens
Qui pert la vieillesse?
Tes enchatemens
Du bien tu devises
Lequel te desplaist
Car tu te deguises
Ainsi qu'il te plaist

Par toi la sourciere
Murmurant ses vers
Nos corps en poussiere
Anime de vers
La lune ensanglate
Et fait remonter
L'eau precipitante
Et les monts sauter

La langue s'asseure
De meriter loz
Si elle demeure
Muette en son clos
Clos fait de dens fortes
Où en serre elle est

[16v]

Venomous tongue,
The husband violates
His most virtuous faith
By means of you;
You abandon
The modest virgin
To a lustful lecher,
O you lewd whore!

Who ruins the young?
Your seductions.
Who ruins old age?
Your enchantments.
You falsely converse about the good,
Which you despise,
Because you disguise yourself
As much as it pleases you.

Through you the witch,
Whispering her spells,
revives with worms
Our dusty corpses.
Your tongue bloodies the moon,
And makes the waterfall rise
Upwards;
It also makes the mountains leap.

The tongue makes sure
To merit praise,
If it remains
Mute in its domain.
This domain is made of strong teeth
Where it is enclosed[1]

---

[1] This domain is the mouth.

[17r]

Comme entre deux portes
Luy servans d'arrest                                    17

La fiere meurtriere
Secretement fait
Que pleine est la biere
De ceux qu'ell'defait
Le ius qu'elle cache
En un petit bout
Si elle le crache
Empoisonne tout

Pourtant j'ay grand doute
Que ton oraison
Poulin ne soit toute
Toute trahison
Car un mercenaire
Du Turc ne craint point
Pour gain de defaire
Le corps à Christ ioint

Si donques ô sire
Ce troupeau te plaist
Ta main le retire
De mort ou il est
Et auz bords estranges
De chascune mer
Tes hautes louanges
Fairons escumer

Ej

[17r]

Like two gates
Shutting it in.

This proud killer
Secretly makes sure
That full is the casket
Of those it undoes.
The juice it hides
In a small phial
Will poison everything
If it spits it.

However, I do truly fear
That your oration,
Poulin, is only
Full of treachery.
For a mercenary
Of the Turks does not fear
To spoil for his own gain
The body joined with Christ.

So, O Lord, if
You love our flock[1]
May your hand protect it
From certain death.
And by the foreign shores
Of every sea
Your high praise
Will sound.[2]

---

[1] Traditional theme of God as the good pastor.

[2] The original verb "escumer" (to foam) is a play on the topic of the sea. Just like the sea inevitably produces foam, through the constant movement of tides, the Waldensians will endlessly praise the Lord for his benevolence.

[17v]

D'opede le chœur le Syndique & le maire

### D'opede

A fin que Poulin mieux paracheve son œuvre
Et que nul de ceux cy oisif ne le descoeuvre
Je les vay empescher à deduire leur foy
Amis il n'est besoin que nous allions au Roy
Si vous me déclarez ce qui est en ce rolle
Je vous escouteray sans dire une parolle

### Le Chœur

Escoutez tous souldars Gendarmes regimens
Comme Dieu par ses faits parolle & sacremens
Qui sont de sa clarté les trois evidens signes
Se manifeste à ceux qui s'en sentent indignes

### Le Syndique

L'escu de nostre foy nostre victoire est tel
Qu'au seul Dieu nous croyons qui seul est immortel

### Le maire

Au Dieu qui seul est Dieu distinct en trois personnes
Qui tout de rien a fait & n'a fait qu'œuvres bonnes

### Le Syndique

Au Dieu qui de trois doits ballançant ce grand tout
Le roule egalement de l'un à l'autre bout

### Le maire

Au Dieu qui a lié d'une rondeur egalle
De toutes pars en soy ceste tant grosse balle

*Tragedy of the Sack of Cabrières*  143

[17v]

D'Opède, the Chorus, the Syndic, and the Mayor

D'Opède
So that Poulin might better complete his work,
And so that none of them discover who he truly is,
I will detain them in speaking of their faith.
Friends, we have no need to go to the king.
If you expose the principles of your religion to me here,
I will listen without saying a thing.

The Chorus
Do listen, O you mercenaries, soldiers, officers![1]
You will see how God with his deeds, his words, and his sacraments,
Which are the three undeniable signs of his brilliance,
Will present himself to those who feel unworthy!

The Syndic
The shield of our faith, our victory, is such
That in the one God we believe, he who alone is immortal.

The Mayor
In the God[2] who is the only God, distinct in three persons,[3]
Who created everything from the void, and only created good things.

The Syndic
In the God who, with three fingers, holding up the whole world,
Can make it move from one end to the other.

The Mayor
In the God who shaped in perfect roundness,
From all parts, such a great sphere.

---

[1] A "gendarme" was a heavily armed soldier on horseback; "regimens" here does not have the sense of the modern English "regiment," but rather that of "leaders, governors," hence my translation by "officers."

[2] The use of this singular expression ("in the God") must be understood from the very goal of this intertwined profession of faith. The God they worship and adore is the one who does all of these actions, by contrast, probably, to a "reappropriation" of God by the Catholics, who would, for the Waldensians, bind his works to their will. For clearer understanding, the reader could add "we believe" before these words.

[3] The holy trinity of God: Father, Son, and Holy Ghost.

### Le Syndique
Au Dieu qui tient unis par accordans discors
Les grands membres qui sont divers en ce grands corps

### Le maire
Au Dieu qui fait virer & sans cesse desvuyde

*Tragedy of the Sack of Cabrières*                                          145

The Syndic
In the God who keeps together, in compatible dissonance,
The great and diverse limbs[1] in this great body.

The Mayor
In the God, thanks to whom turns and rolls,

---

[1] An obvious reference to the notion of the body politic. A play, also, on "membre" that, in French, means either "limb" or "member."

[18r]

Au tour de deux pivets le rond de ce grand vuide         18

             Le Syndique
Au Dieu qui quand il veut tout le monde estonner
Ne fait sinon qu'un peu sa voix haute entonner

             Le maire
Au Dieu qui fait nager sur les monts dedans l'onde
Les Dauphins de la mer s'il en leve la bonde

             Le Syndique
Au Dieu qui la mer change en beaux champs defrichez
Empoudrant dans le fonds les poissons dessechez

             Le maire
Au Dieu qui jusqu'au ciel la vallée emmontaigne
Et le mont sourcilleux applanit en Campaigne

             Le Syndique
Au Dieu qui à la fin bruslera l'univers
Et sauvera les siens en perdant les pervers

             Le maire
Au Dieu qui hait peche pour qui la Terre endure
Bruslant tantost de chauld & tantost de froidure

             Le Syndique
Soit qu'approchant la Torche il allonge les jours
Ou soit que l'eslongnant il les rongne plus courts

             Le maire
Quand la terre est de soif beante & embrasée
Il l'abbreuve & refait de sa pluye & rosée

             Le Syndique
Fait elle trop la brave? Il la despouille aussi
Luy ridant l'estomach en glace tout transi

                Eij

# Tragedy of the Sack of Cabrières

[18r]

Around two pivots, the sphere of this great void.

The Syndic
In the God who, when he wants to astound all people,
Only has to intone with his loud voice.

The Mayor
In the God who can make dolphins swim over
The mountains if he raises the waters.

The Syndic
In the God who turns the sea into beautiful, clear fields,
Covering the desiccated fishes on the seafloor with powdery dust.

The Mayor
In the God who turns the valley into a sky-high mountain,
And who levels the haughty bluff into flat countryside.[1]

The Syndic
In the God who, in the end, will burn the universe,
Save his people, and destroy the corrupt.

The Mayor
In the God who hates sin, for which the Earth suffers
At times burning heat and at times dire cold.

The Syndic
When he brings forth the light, he lengthens days;
When he takes it back, he trims them shorter.

The Mayor
When the Earth is arid and suffering from thirst,
He quenches and covers it with rain and dew.

The Syndic
Is the Earth too lavishly dressed? He will strip it down,
Stiffening its belly, numbed by ice.

---

[1] See Isa. 40:4, "Every valley shall be exalted and every mountain and hill brought low; the crooked places shall be made straight and the rough places smooth."

[18v]

Le M.
De neige il l'enfarine & la teste chenue
Il couvre de frimas où seroit toute nue

Le S.
Quant au poisson il fait un marbre de son eau
L'empierrant vif dedans ainsi qu'en un tombeau

Le M.
C'est luy qui seul refond ce marbre en son mol estre
Et fait d'un tel Chrystal l'eau coulante renaistre

Le S.
Quand la bise enferrée en mille chants nouveaux
Par Zephire il enchante à l'ennuy les oiseaux

Le M.
C'est luy qui d'un regard de son grand œil du monde
Ceste mere de tous rend chascun an feconde

Le S.
De ses fleurs diaprée en cent mille couleurs
Puis grosse de tous fruits engendrez de leurs fleurs

Le M.
Qu'il garde & fait meurir jusqu'au vineux Automne
Lors sa main liberale à tout le monde en donne

Le S.
Vray que pour nos meffaits quelquefois Souverain
Tu fais le ciel de fer & la terre d'airain

Le M.
Bref tes faits ô Dieu sont faits si admirables
Qu'autre n'en feit n'en fait n'en faira de semblables

*Tragedy of the Sack of Cabrières*

[18v]

The M.
He powders it with snow, and covers its whitened head
With frost, where it is uncovered.

The S.
As for the fish, he turns its water into marble,
Immuring it alive inside, as in a tomb.

The M.
It is he, and only he, who brings this marble back to its liquid state
And from that crystal, running water is reborn.

The S.
From the cold wind, adorned with a thousand new songs,
He enchants Zephyr, disturbing the birds.[1]

The M.
It is he who, with a gaze of his great eye,
Fecundates every year this mother of us all:

The S.
Richly festooned with flowers of one hundred thousand colors,
Then big with the fruits that came from these flowers,

The M.
Which he maintains and ripens until comes winey Autumn,
When his benevolent hand shares them with everyone.

The S.
It is true that, for our misdeeds, Lord, you sometimes
Turn the sky into iron and our land into brass.[2]

The M.
In short, your deeds, O God, are such admirable deeds
That no one has done, does, or ever will do.

---

[1] Zephyr, the Greek god of the west wind.
[2] See Lev. 26:19: "I will break the pride of your power; I will make your heavens like iron and your earth like bronze."

Le S.
Par les seuls faits pourtant du tout bon toutpuissant
Qui est l'enfant d'Adam de son Dieu cognoissant?

*Tragedy of the Sack of Cabrières* 151

The S.
Still, by the sole deeds of the all benevolent and all powerful one,
Who is the son of Adam, who recognizes his God?

[19r]

19

### Le M.
En lieu d'y veoir bien clair de soy nostre nature
(Ignorant animal) pleine est de nuict obscure

### Le S.
L'aveugle ainsi ne peut du jeu de l'acteur
Bien qu'il soit au thatre en estre spectateur

### Le M.
Ainsi ne peut le sourd ce qu'on lui dit entendre
Ny l'impotent manchot ce qu'on luy donne prendre

### Le S.
Pourtant aussi d'ailleurs Dieu a l'homme esclairé
S'estant son createur & sauveur declairé
Par le miel distillant de sa divine bouche

### Le M.
Donc si divinement tous ses sens il luy touche
Qu'il cognoit comme Dieu l'avoit au plus beau lieu
De la terre en honneur mis comme un demy-Dieu
Car quand il eut portrait sur sa divine idée
Sa Corne d'abondance fut en luy si vuidée
Qu'il n'y avoit un tel chef d'œuvre sous les cieux

### Le S.
Il l'avoit tout comblé des presens de son mieux
Soit de sa crainte, amour, iustice, cognoissance,
Soit de sagesse, force, & vraye obeissance.

*Tragedy of the Sack of Cabrières*                                                              153

[19r]

The M.
Rather than having a clear view of himself, of our nature
(Ignorant beast) is blinded by a dark night.

The S.
Of the actor's performance, the blind man cannot
Be the spectator, even though he is in the theater.

The M.
Likewise, the deaf cannot hear what is said to him,
Just like the one-armed man cannot grab what is given to him.

The S.
However, God has also enlightened mankind,
As its creator and its revealed savior,
Through the honey distilled by his divine mouth. [1]

The M.
Therefore, if man is heavenly touched in all its senses by him,
May he acknowledge how he was put by God as a demi-God
In the most beautiful place on Earth; [2]
For when he designed it according to his divine plan, [3]
He poured his cornucopia on mankind,
Because there was no such masterpiece under the heavens.

The S.
He blessed mankind with all his best gifts,
Either fear of God, love, justice, knowledge,
Or wisdom, strength, and true obedience,

---

[1] There is here an obvious comparison between the benevolent words of God and the malicious, ill-fated words of d'Opède and Poulin.

[2] A continuation of the metaphor of Adam; the "most beautiful place on Earth" here is then the Garden of Eden.

[3] A reference to Gen. 1:27: "So God created man in His own image; in the image of God He created him; male and female He created them."

## Le M.

Ou soit d'authorité & d'un exquis sçavoir
Soit d'un pur jugement soit d'un livre pouvoir
De tenir droit le cours de toutes ses pensées,
Œuvres & volontés saintement compassées

## Le S.

Vous comteriez plustost les celestes flambeaux
Les pleurs de l'occean & le bords de ses eaux          Eiij

*Tragedy of the Sack of Cabrières*

The M.
Or authority and exquisite knowledge,
Or a pure judgment, or the power of a book
To organize the stream of his thoughts,
Works, and wills devoutly arranged.[1]

The S.
But you would more easily count the celestial torches,
The tears of the ocean, and the shores of his waters,

---

[1] Probably the Bible.

[19v]

Que les biens que receut ceste fange animée
De l'autheur qui l'avoist si richement formée

Le M.

Ô largesse! ô faveur! ô libéralité!

Le S.

Ô Adam plus qu'ingrat! quelle desloyauté
D'avoir creu l'ennemy de tout l'humain lignage
Et sacrilege estaint du Dieu vivant l'image!

Le M.

Il s'est faict ignorant esclave du peché
De son Dieu adversaire à Sathan attaché
N'ayant pas seulement du bien la seule envie.

Le S.

En tout vice plongé il ne peut en sa vie
Produire que peché peché le fruit de mort
Comme engendre le vers la charrongne d'un mort.

Le M.

Peche bouillone en luy & la race il y plonge
Qui s'en emboit ainsi comme d'humeur l'esponge

Le S.

Tout la parfait change de sa perfection
En la perversité de sa corruption
Il ne retient plus rien de ses divines graces
Sinon (outre tout mal) du bien perdu les traces

Le M.

Comme quand de l'orgueil d'un superbe Chasteau
Qui les cieux menaçoit d'un haut rocher en l'eau
Ne reste qu'un bourbier sepulchre de ruines
Couverte d'une horreur de ronces & d'espines

*Tragedy of the Sack of Cabrières*

157

[19v]

Rather than the gifts granted to this animated dust,
From the author who so richly crafted it!

The M.
O generosity! O favor! O benevolence!

The S.
O Adam, you more than ingrate! What disloyalty
It was to believe the enemy of all humankind[1]
And, sacrilege! To have extinguished the image of the living God!

The M.
This ignorant man enslaved himself to sin,
Enemy of its God, attached to Satan,
Without even the desire for goodness!

The S.
All submerged into vice, in his life man[2]
Can only generate sin. Sin! The fruit of death,
Just as worms are engendered by corpses.

The M.
Sin boils inside mankind, and engulfs in it
The race that inebriates itself, like a sponge soaked in moisture.

The S.
All that was perfect turns from its perfection
Into the perversity of its corruption.
Nothing remains of its godly graces
Except (beside all evil) only traces of the good it lost.

The M.
Just as when, from the pride of a once splendid castle,
Which scared heavens from a high rock in the water,
Only remains a quagmire, a tomb in ruins,
Covered with horrible thorns and brambles.

---

[1] The "humain lignage" refers not only to mankind as it was when the original sin happened, but also, and foremost, to its descendants.

[2] All these lines always use the pronoun "il" here for mankind. Repeating it would make the evolution of the attacks harder to follow, which made me add "mankind" to some of the verses in order to make them intelligible.

[20r]

Le S.                    20

Pour s'estre malheureux de tout bien despouillé
Et pour s'estre meschant en tout peché souillé
Dieu juste l'a jugé à la mort eternelle
Et si fait grace encor au condamné rebelle

Le M.

Grace par Jesuchrist qui pour cela s'est fait
Semence de la femme & a peche defait
Et la mort, par la mort satisfaisant au Pere

Le S.

Par la mort qui occit l'homicide vipere

Le M.

Par la mort qui seule est l'acquit de nos forfaits

Le S.

Par la mort qui seule est notre rançon & paix

Le M.

Par la mort qui seule est de la mort la victoire

Le S.

Par la mort qui seule est de tous Chrestiens la gloire

Le M.

Par la mort qui seule est le sacrifice entier
Qui seul l'homme refait des hauts cieux heretier

Le S.

Par la mort qui seule est divinement puissante
D'abolir & la coulpe & la peine sanglante

Le M.

Par la mort qui seule est le vray & seul moyen
Pourquoy Dieu de son droit fait grace & n'en perd rien

*Tragedy of the Sack of Cabrières*     159

[20r]

The S.
Because man, O wretched soul, stripped himself of all good,
And because he, evil!, is soiled with sin,
God sentenced mankind with eternal death,
And yet pardoned the rebellious prisoner.

The M.
Grace by Jesus Christ, who for this became
Offspring of a woman, and vanquished sin
And death, thus repaying his father through death.[1]

The S.
With his death he slayed the deadly viper.

The M.
With his death, which alone is forgiveness for our sins.

The S.
With his death, which is the price of our peace.

The M.
With his death, which is the sole victory over Death.

The S.
With his death, which alone is glory for all Christians.

The M.
With his death, which is the only sacrifice
That restores mankind as the rightful heir to heaven.

The S.
With his death, which alone is the divine power
That abolishes guilt and bloody punishment.

The M.
With his death, the true and only means
Through which God grants his grace without losing anything.

---

[1] Death as the pathway to eternal life, a Christian trope, here to be seen through the Protestant lens of predestination.

## Le S.

Car justice au peché innocement cruelle
Et la grace au pecheur saintement paternelle
Ont le peché destruit & le pecheur sauvé
Par ceste mort ou Dieu juste & bon est trouvé

Eiiij

The S.
For justice, innocently cruel to sin,
And grace, holy in its paternal care for the sinner,
Have destroyed sin, and saved the sinner,
Through Death, in which our just and good God we will find.

[20v]

Le M.

O divine bonté! ô sagesse infinie
Ô abysme d'amour qui par l'ignominie
D'une maudite croix en quittant le forfait
Au droit de ta justice entiere a satisfait

Le S.

Pere tu es la source & la cause premiere
Du salut des esleus et ton fils la matiere
La Foy est l'instrument par lequel le S. Esprit
Nous le fait recevoir de toy en Iesuschrist

Le M.

Estant ainsi sauvez par la divine grace
Il faut qu'a Dieu chascun obeissance face
Non pas en la façon que l'enragé bigot
Invente en son cerveau pour se monstrer devot.

Le S.

Tout service forgé est devant Dieu infame
Plus que devant nos yeux les draps souillez de femme

Le M.

Combien de fois Seigneur as tu dit en ta loy
Si je suis vostre Dieu mon peuple servez moy
Sans rien changer ou mettre à ce que je commande
L'obéir seul me plait & non pas vostre offrande

Le S.

Je veux dit il aussi que prompts de cœur & main
Vous secouriez heureux chascun vostre prochain
Vous fait il mille torts? pour le mal bien luy faites
Ce sont de charité mes saintes loix parfaites

Le M.

Helas qui est celuy qui en a le pouvoir?
Pouvoir! ains qui en peut le seul desir avoir

*Tragedy of the Sack of Cabrières*  163

[20v]

The M.
O divine goodness! O infinite wisdom!
O infinite depth of love that, paying the debt by the
Ignominy of an accursed cross,
Has satisfied the claim of your entire justice!

The S.
Father, you are the source and primary cause
Of the salvation of the chosen ones, and your son is its substance;
Faith is the means through which the Holy Ghost
Helps us to receive him through you in Jesus Christ.[1]

The M.
Hence, saved by divine grace,
Everybody must swear obedience to God,
But not as the enraged bigot
Invents it in his head, to feign devotion.[2]

The S.
Any contrived service is repugnant to God,
Even more to our eyes than the soiled sheets of a woman.

The M.
How many times, Lord, have you heralded in your law,
"If I am your God, serve me, O my people!
Without changing or adding to what I command;
Your obedience, not your offerings, is all that pleases me."

The S.
I also wish, he says, that with prompt heart and hands,
You each happily save your neighbors.
Does he do you a thousand wrongs? For every ill, give him a good.
Such are my perfect holy laws of charity.

The M
Alas, who has the power to do so?
Power? Rather, who can even have such a desire?

---

[1]  The trinity of God: Father, Son, and Holy Spirit.
[2]  Believing must be in the heart, and for oneself, and not a spectacle for others.

## [21r]

21

Pource la loy condamne equitablement l'homme
Debteur à son Seigneur de la totale somme
Que par sa seule faute il ne scauroit payer

Le S.

Pource qu'il a perdu iusqu'au dernier denier
Tout ce qu'il avoit eu de la bonté divine
À son œuvre enrichir prodiguement benigne

Le M.

Comment payra il donc? qu'il aille à Jesuchrist
Qui cancellant la debte & le contract escrit
Mourant l'a dechiré en la faveur du pouvre
Qui par Christ acquité son bien perdu recouvre.

Le S.

Sommes nous derechef sous le peché plongés
Allos à Iesuchrist pour estre soulagez
Et par son Saint Esprit de nous fiante et ordures
Saintement il faira nouvelles creatures

Le M.

Allons allons à luy & nous y puyserons
Mille fois plus de bien que nous ne jugerons
Nous defaillir allons à luy de bon courage
Car plus que reparée il a de Dieu l'image
Joignnant en un corps l'homme & la divinité

*Tragedy of the Sack of Cabrières*

[21r]

For the law condemns equitably the man
Who is in debt to his lord, of the whole sum
That he will not be able to pay, by his own fault.[1]

The S.
For this, he lost to his last penny;[2]
All that he received from divine goodness,
Prodigally generous to enrich his work.

The M.
How then will he pay? He should go to Jesus Christ
Who cancelled[3] the debt, and the written contract
That he tore apart with his death, for the sake of the poor
Who recovered his lost property thanks to Christ.

The S.
Are we yet again drowned in sin?
Let us go to Jesus Christ to be relieved
And through his Holy Spirit, we who are excrement and waste,[4]
He will turn us into new creatures with his holiness.

The M.
Let us go to him! From him we will draw
A thousand times more good than we think
We are lacking; let us courageously go to him,
For he has more than restored the image of God,
Rejoining in one body man and divinity.[5]

---

[1] A possible reference to Rom. 11:35, "Who has ever given to God, that God should repay them?"

[2] The original term of "denier" has a translation of "denarius" (plural "denarii"). However, the *OED* itself states that they stand for the equivalent of pennies, which is why I used it here.

[3] The original word, "canceller" comes from the Latin word "cancellare," which means "cross out." Here, the image is of Jesus physically removing the debt through his death, like a debt is crossed out of a contract, which the end of the line underlines.

[4] "Fiante" is a bird dropping, or guano. However, the use of "waste" better represents the general meaning of the sentence, in which man is nothing but waste before the power of God, who forgives his actions and gives him back his formidable love.

[5] Reference to the Holy Trinity.

Le S.

Arriere donc d'Adam premiere dignité
Puisque perdre il t'a peu par sa cheute mortelle
Mais celle que Christ donne est sans fin eternelle
L'emphyteose estant en commis expiré
Adam merveilleux gain de sa perte a tiré.

Fj

The S.
Away then, first dignity of Adam![1]
For he caused your ruin in his mortal fall.
But that which was given by Christ is eternal without end,
Since the emphyteusis[2] expired:
Adam profited magnificently by his loss.[3]

---

[1] The snake, here representing the devil.

[2] A very long lease; here put in reference to Adam having finished his stay and his punishment, and finally being able to benefit from eternal life. God does not punish forever.

[3] The theme of "felix culpa," the happy fault of Adam and Eve that in spite of its horror, eventually paved the way for man to gain redemption and reclaim its place back in heaven. See Sean A. Otto, "Felix Culpa: The Doctrine of Original Sin as Doctrine of Hope in Aquinas's *Summa Contra Gentiles,*" *Heythrop Journal* (2009): 781–92.

[21v]

## Le M.

Pour ne le perdre plus Christ par son sacrifice
Incessamēnt nous rend Dieu son pere propice
Nous ayant consacrez tous sacrificateurs
Pour offrir en son nom du profond de nos cœurs
A son Pere non point de bœufs mouton et chievres
Mais en Esprit & foy les bouveaux de nos leures

## Le S.

Encor'icy faut il que le Saint Esprit soit
Celuy qui dans nos cœurs les prieres concoit

## Le M.

Il nous faut craindre Dieu l'aimant d'amour non vaine
Nous faut aimer le bien le vice avoir en haine

## Le S.

Nous met sa loy au cœur l'engrave & l'y escrit
Nous nettoye arrousez du sang de Jesuchrist

## Le M.

Et nourrit de son corps nos ames affamées
Pour estre de la mort eternelle sauvées

## Le S.

Nous appliquant tout Christ ainsi qu'Il est le corps
Des umbres de la loy pour nous animer morts

## Le M.

À fin que conduisions nostre mortelle course
À l'honneur du Seigneur de tous nos biens la source

[21v]

The M.
So that man might not fall again, Christ through his sacrifice
Constantly makes God propitious to us.
He sanctified us as priests[1]
To offer, in his name, from the depth of our hearts,
To his father, no oxen, sheep, or goats,
But rather, in spirit and in faith, the calves of our lips.[2]

The S.
Still, the Holy Spirit must be
That which engenders prayers in our hearts.

The M.
We must fear God, yet love him not in vain.
We must love good and have hatred for vice.

The S.
He engraved and inscribed his law in our hearts;
He washes us in the blood of Jesus Christ and purifies us,

The M.
And feeds from his body our famished souls
To save them from eternal death,

The S.
Giving ourselves over to Christ, since he is the body
Of the shadows of law, to animate us when we are dead,

The M.
So that we directly owe our mortal life
To the honor of God, source of all our good.

---

[1] The word "sacrificateur" designates a priest who was charged to sacrifice animals. Here, words and propagating his deeds are the only sacrifices that God demands.". The theme of propagation of the real faith was a common trope in Protestant literature and will appear throughout the text, notably in the end. The idea was that since they were persecuted, making the movement grow would prevent the Catholics from wiping it out.

[2] The two verses seem to be a reference to Deut. 14:4, "These are the animals which you may eat: the ox, the sheep, the goat." The "veal" of their lips, the tender meat of their faith and spirit, is what the real believers must offer to God. The French word "veau," from which "bouveau" can be traced, means both "veal" and "calf."

D'ope.

Mais qui est cestuy là qui s'en vient droit à moy?
Est ce Poulin? oui, c'est bien luy je le voy
Je vous orray tantost, si quelque chose reste.

*Tragedy of the Sack of Cabrières*

D'Ope.
But who is this fellow, who is coming straight toward me?
Is this Poulin? Yes, it is whom I see.
I will hear you immediately, if there is something to say.

[22r]

22

Ô vilains dangereux sept fois plus que la peste
Je vous feray mourir par tourmens si cruels
Que Phalaris jamais n'en inventa de tels.

Le Cœur

Telephe ne peut onques
Trouver allegrement
Ne remedes quelconques
Au mal de son tourment
Sinon que de sa lame
Le Grec cruel humain
La vieille playe entame
Ja faite de sa main

Ainsi, ô langue bleme
Qui n'a guere elancois
Tes dards contre toy mesme
Si fort t'en meurtrissois
Qu'ores nulle momie
Ne t'en peut secourir
Par ta palinodie
Seule te peux guarir

*Tragedy of the Sack of Cabrières* 173

[22r]

O villains, seven times more dangerous than the plague!
I shall kill you by crueler torments,
Than Phalaris[1] had ever invented.

The Chorus

Telephus was never able
To find solace
Nor any remedy
For the agony of his torment,
Unless if, with his blade,
This cruel Greek fellow
Reopens the old wound
That he once inflicted on himself.[2]

Thus, O pale tongue
Who seldom threw
Your own spears against yourself,
You were hurting yourself so much
That presently no ointment
Can save you.
Only your palinode[3]
Can cure you.

---

[1] Sicilian tyrant, known for his cruelty. The torture method known as the brazen bull (a hollow bull statue, with a door on its side, into which people were thrown and literally roasted to death) is also attributed to him.

[2] Son of Hercules and Auge, and king of Tegea. He was injured by Achille's spear on the way to Troy: "Telephus, son of Hercules and Auge, is said to have been wounded by Achilles in battle with the spear of Chiron" (Hyginus, *Fables*, trans. Mary Grant, Theoi Classical Texts Library, https://www.theoi.com/Text/HyginusFabulae3.html). The wound was uncurable and caused Telephus great pain. An oracle told him that only the blade that had injured him could cure him, "So Achilles healed him by scraping off the rust of his Pelian spear" (Apollodorus, *Epitome*, trans. and ed. James George Frazer, Perseus Digital Library, http://www.perseus.tufts.edu/hopper/text?doc=Perseus:abo:tlg, 0548,002:e:3:20).

[3] Rhetorical retractation of previously stated arguments. The Chorus here encourages those who uttered the fallacious words spoken in its previous declaration to recognize their foulness and to retract themselves.

La plante dont Mercure
Arma le fin Gregois
Avoit ceste nature
Que Circe de sa voix
Vers remachés ne poudres
Malfaire ne pouvoit
Ne de jus ne de foudres
À celuy qui l'avoit

Fij

*Tragedy of the Sack of Cabrières*                                        175

The plant with which Mercury
Armed the cunning Greek,
Was of such nature that
Circe,[1] with her voice,
Could not do harm with it,
Neither with words or powder,
Nor with potions or spells
To whomever had taken it.[2]

---

[1] This stanza is a reference to the *Odyssey*, book 10. When Ulysses and his companions land on Aeaea, half of his group gets trapped by the sorceress and changed into pigs. Ulysses stumbles upon Mercury ("But Hermes met me, with his golden wand, / Barring the way—a boy whose lip was downy / In the first bloom of manhood, so he seemed," vv. 295–97) and recognizes him. The latter gives him a magic plant ("He bent down glittering for the magic plant / And pulled it up, black root and milky flower / —a molü in the language of the gods," vv.331–33). All references come from Homer, *The Odyssey*, trans. Robert Fitzgerald (New York: Farrar, Strauss, and Giroux, 1998).

[2] This reference will be used later on by Ronsard in his *Continuation*, where the moly is supposed to prevent the Protestants from tricking the Catholics: "O seigneur tout puissant, ne mets point en oubly / D'envoyer un Mercure avecque le Moly / Vers ce noble seigneur" (*Œuvres complètes*, ed. Cohen, 2:556) (O all powerful lord, please do not forget / To send Mercury with his moly / To this noble lord).

[22v]

Tel Moly que la langue
Ne fut onc sous le Ciel
Le fruit de sa harangue
Est un fruit tout de miel
Qui succrant les oreilles
Faire ouyr voire aux morts
Ô Dieu les grands merveilles
Des tes divins thresors.

Nulle autre ne revele
Le salut precieux
Ne l'amour paternele
Qu'en ton fils glorieux
Tu monstres a nous hommes
Plains de desloyauté
Qui tousiours ingrats sommes
Envers ta grand bonté

Sans elle à l'Evangile
Qui le souverain bien
Sainctement nous distille
Ne croiroit le chrestien
Cent mille piperies
Des affronteurs caphards
Ne seroient point haïes
Ne leurs masques ne fards

Un bien petit boys guide
Ca & là les grands naufs
Un petit mords de bride

*Tragedy of the Sack of Cabrières* 177

[22v]
A tongue like the moly
Never lived under the sky:
The fruit of its speech
Is a honeyed fruit,
Which, sweet to the ears,
Allows the dead to hear the truth,
O God, of the great wonders
Of your divine treasures.

Nothing else reveals
The precious salvation
Or the paternal love
That in your glorious son
You showed us, men
Full of disloyalty,
Who are always ungrateful
Toward your great goodness.

Without it, the Gospel,
Which its sovereign goodness
So holily to us distills,
Wouldn't be believed by Christians;
A hundred thousand trickeries
From the contentious hypocrites[1]
Would not be despised,
And neither would their masks and their artifices.

A very small rudder[2]
Can guide very big ships;
The very small bit of a bridle

---

[1] "Caphard" here cannot be translated as cockroach, as this word was not used to designate the insect in the Blattodea order until after the sixteenth century. The original, ancient meaning of "hypocrite, foul" must be used here.

[2] The original word is a metonymy for the matter of the rudder.

[23r]

23

Retient les fiers chevaux
Et la foible tenaille
Le gros barreau de fer
Que le forgeur entaille
Et puis fait rechauffer.

La langue ainsi gouverne
Petite qu'elle soit
Tout le monde & prosterne
Quiconq nous deçoit
Sans elle nulle ville
N'a esté ne seroit
Ne l'arme en soc utile
Changée on ne verroit

Elle seule discorde
Meine & les mutins ords
Tous de chaine & de corde
Les bras liez au corps
Par elle ils se bannissent
De toute cruauté
Et à la paix s'unissent
Contraints de volonté

L'ire l'homme surmonte
Et le fait furieux
Mais la langue le domte
Et le rend gracieux
Elle à David retire                    Fiij

[23r]

Restrains proud steeds,
As fragile pincers
Hold a big bar of iron
That the blacksmith cuts
And then heats once more.

The tongue governs,
As insignificant as it is,
The whole world, and knocks down
Anyone who tricks us.
Without it, no city
Would have been or would be.
Neither would we have seen the weapon
Turned into the useful plowshare.[1]

Only it brings discord,
And its horrible mutineers,
All in chains and hobbled,
With their arms bound to their bodies.
Through them, they banish
All cruelty,
And unite in peace,
Constrained by will as they are.

Man is overcome by anger,
And becomes furious;
But words tame him,
And make him gracious again.
It took the weapons

---

[1] See note 61.

[23v]

Les armes de la main
Ia ja prest à occire
Nabal trop inhumain

À la peur couppe l'aile
Luy faisant tenir bon
D'une victoire belle
Lui monstrant le guerdon
Au contraire elle glace
Des plus cruels le cœur
Leur palissant la face
D'une fuite d'honneur

Qu'au prochain on ne nuyse
Violant l'équité
Par la langue est apprise
La loy de Charite
D'elle est le mariage
Lien du genre humain
Qui estend d'aage en aage
Nostre passé demain

Si le corps navré seigne
En danger de mourir
La langue nous enseigne
Comm'il le faut guairir
Par celle d'Hippocrate
S'appliquent tous les jours
Au cerveau foye & race
Mille presens secours.

*Tragedy of the Sack of Cabrières*

181

[23v]

From the hands of David
As he was ready to slay
The inhuman Nabal.[1]

They cut the wings of fear,
Making it hold tight:
Showing it the reward
Of a beautiful victory.
On the contrary, language freezes
The hearts of the cruelest men,
Turns their face pale
As honor flees.

You shall not harm your neighbor,[2]
And thus not violate justice:
For the law of charity
Is taught through words.
From them come marriage,
Bond of humankind
That extends throughout the ages,
Our past to tomorrow.

If an injured body is bleeding
And in danger of dying,
Words teach us
How to heal it.
Thanks to the words of Hippocrates[3]
Everyday are applied
To the brain, the liver, and the spleen
A thousand remedies.

---

[1] Nabal was a Calebite who insulted David before he was king. David remembers it and vows to kill him. However, after Nabal's wife pleads for her husband, and after David realizes that he would be sinning if he killed Nabal, he decides to spare him (see 1 Sam. 25).

[2] An obvious reference to commandments 9 and 10: "You shall not bear false witness against your neighbor. / You shall not covet your neighbor's house; you shall not covet your neighbor's wife, nor his male servant, nor his female servant, nor his ox, nor his donkey, nor anything that is your neighbor's" (Exod. 20:16–17).

[3] Hippocrates, Greek physician, the father of Western medicine.

[24r]

La langue outre console                         24
Le mortel tourmenté
Du goust de la parolle
Le pouvre est sustenté
Et les cœurs des debiles
En sont fortifiez.
Les vefves & pupilles
Gardez de torts & grief

Par elle un des prophetes
Multiplie vingt pains
Dont cent bouches refaites
Plus en reste en leurs mains
D'elle l'huile regorge
Le rachapt des mineurs
Retirez de la gorge
Des cruels crediteurs

La femme Sunamite
Son fils mort vivre voit
Par une voix beneite
De l'hoste qu'elle avoit
Par famine opressée
Ayant erré sept ans
Par la langue adressée
Au roy receut ses champs

Roy dont David fut pere
Roy sur tous triomphant
A la dolente mere                     Fiiij

*Tragedy of the Sack of Cabrières*     183

[24r]

Besides, language consoles
The tormented mortal.
With the taste of the word of God
The poor man is sustained,
And the hearts of the weak
Are fortified;
The widows and orphans
Are protected from wrongdoing and grief.

Through language, one of the prophets
Multiplies twenty loaves,
with which a hundred mouths are filled,
And they have more left in their hands;[1]
Oil flows from language
And protects the miners,
Who are saved
From the greedy maw of their creditors.

The Shunammite woman[2]
Sees her dead son alive,
Thanks to a blessed voice
Of the host she welcomed.
Oppressed by hunger,
He who erred during seven years,
Thanks to the words addressed to the king,
Recovered his fields.[3]

King, of whom David was the father,[4]
King, triumphing over all,
To the doleful mother

---

[1] See 2 Kings 4:42–43: "Then a man came from Baal Shalisha, and brought the man of God bread of the firstfruits, twenty loaves of barley bread, and newly ripened grain in his knapsack. And he said, 'Give it to the people, that they may eat.' / But his servant said, 'What? Shall I set this before one hundred men?' He said again, 'Give it to the people, that they may eat; for thus says the Lord: "They shall eat and have some left over."'"

[2] The whole passage is a reference to the deeds of the prophet Elisha, who resurrected the son of a Shunammite woman, in 2 Kings 4:37: "So she went in, fell at his feet, and bowed to the ground; then she picked up her son and went out"

[3] A possible reference to the seven-year Tribulation.

[4] King Solomon.

[24v]

Ta voix rend vif l'enfant
Et l'enfant mort à celle
Qui au vif n'avoit rien
Ayant sous son aisselle
De nuit estaint le sien

Si dru ne court la bise
Les chesnes arracher
Qu'a une voix se brise
L'audace de la chair
Si qu'en laissant le vice
Le pecheur n'est plus tel
Ou bien sans qu'il guairisse
Il chet d'un coup mortel

Quand Nathan vitupere
Au nom de Dieu David
Le meurtrier adultere
Se repentir il vit
La seule voix d'Elie
Le double Achab reprit
Les prestres de Bal lie
Qui le peuple meurtrit

*Tragedy of the Sack of Cabrières* 185

[24v]

Your voice gave back her son, alive;
And the dead child
To the one who had not a living one,
Since she had under her arms
At night smothered her own.[1]

If the wind blows so forcefully
That it does uproot oak trees,
May the audacity of flesh
Break thanks to a single voice.
Thus, when he gives up on sinning,
A sinner is no longer one,
Otherwise, without a cure,
He falls from a mortal wound.

When Nathan berates against
David in the name of God,[2]
He saw the adulterous killer
Immediately repent.
The lone voice of Elijah,
Which the treacherous Ahab reproved,
Hindered the priests of Baal,
Who wounded the people;[3]

---

[1] A clear reference to 1 Kings 3:16–28, with the two prostitutes and their sons.

[2] See 2 Sam. 12:1–13, and particularly verse 13: "So David said to Nathan, 'I have sinned against the Lord.' And Nathan said to David, 'The Lord also has put away your sin; you shall not die.'"

[3] See 1 Kings chapters 16 to 20, and the persecution of the prophets of Israel.

À la parole seulle
De Jehu les limiers
Detrenchent en leur gueule Jezabel à quartiers
Et à celle de Pierre
L'hypocrite aumosnier
Tomba tout mort par terre
Et ne fut le dernier

*Tragedy of the Sack of Cabrières*

With a single word
From Jehu, the bloodhounds
Tore Jezebel to pieces in their maws.[1]
With Peter's words,[2]
The hypocritical almsman[3]
Fell on the ground, dead,
And was not the last to do so.

---

[1] 2 Kings 9:35–36. After having Jezebel thrown out of the window, Jehu has his dogs eat her bloody remains: "So they went to bury her, but they found no more of her than the skull and the feet and the palms of her hands. / Therefore they came back and told him. And he said: 'This is the word of the Lord, which He spoke by His servant Elijah the Tishbite, saying: "On the plot of ground at Jezreel dogs shall eat the flesh of Jezebel."'"

[2] Ananias, whose deception with his wife Sapphira (he was hiding money from a land sale) was discovered by Peter, whose words killed him. All these excerpts from the Bible target the power of words, and how they can be used for good or evil deeds; see Acts 5:1–11.

[3] An "aumosnier" was, in the context of the text, the clergyman responsible for giving alms to the poor, and not a chaplain, which is the modern meaning of the word.

[25r]

Et contreignant sa force
Sa douceur en priant                           25
De rendre à Dieu s'efforce
Tout genouil bas ployant
Iusqué aux bords ou le more
Plonge ses noirs cheveux
Elle fait qu'on adore
L'eternel par saints vœus

Elle invite à priere
Le cœur froid sommeillant
Quand priant la premiere
Survient le reveillant
Comme si premier prie
Le Cœur la langue esmeut
Tellement qu'elle crie
Tout ce que le cœur veut

Anne pour estre mere
Du juste Samuel
Emflambant sa priere
D'un vœu continuel
D'ardeur ses levres ouvre
Pour parler maintefois
Son cœur donc se decoeuvre
Et provoque sa voix

Cest accord tant louable
De la langue & du cœur
Le Pechier delectable
Demonstre apres sa fleur                    Gj

[25r]

And controlling his force
His sweetness urged him
To give himself to God
Kneeling down on both knees;
To the shores where the Moor
Plunges his dark hair
Words make people adore
The Eternal by holy vows.

Words invite to prayer
The sleeping cold heart,
As it recites the Prime;[1]
They come and wake it up.
As if the first to pray was
The heart, which stirs the tongue
So much that it shouts
All that the heart wants to hear.

To become the mother
Of the just Samuel, Hannah,
Illuminating her prayer
From an eternal vow,
Opened her lips ardently
To speak many times.
Then, her heart was uncovered
And spurred on her voice.[2]

This praiseworthy accord
Of tongue and heart
Is seen in the delectable peach tree
After it blossoms.

---

[1] One of the prayers of the Liturgy of the Hours, after Lauds.

[2] Hannah, who could not bear a child, addressed a prayer to the Lord, who provided her with Samuel. See 1 Sam. 1:11: "Then she made a vow and said, 'O Lord of hosts, if You will indeed look on the affliction of Your maidservant and remember me, and not forget Your maidservant, but will give Your maidservant a male child, then I will give him to the Lord all the days of his life, and no razor shall come upon his head.'"

[25v]

Car à son fruit ressemble
Le cœur si rondement
Qu'à sa fueille qui tremble
La langue droitement

Ô personnes heureuses
Des quelles pour la mort
Les langues non peureuses
Avec le cœur d'accord
Des reclamer ne craignent
Iesuchrist pour leur Roy
Ne pour tyran se feignent
De declarer leur foy.

C'est ce qu'ont fait sans feinte
Dedans un camp armé
Ces deux d'une voix sainte
Et d'un cœur animé
Ô que leur foy tresample
Qu'on leur oyt prononcer
À vous serve d'exemple
Pour Iesus confesser

Si qu'en paix & en guerre
Toute langue de cœur
Chante dessus la Terre
La loz de sa grandeur
Qui seul sur soy descharge
Les pecheurs accablez
Les rendans (douce charge!)
De sa grace comblez

[25v]

For the heart resembles its fruit
So perfectly,
As words also mirror
Its trembling leaves.

O happy people
Whose tongues,
Not fearful of death,
In accord with the heart,
Do not fear to claim
Jesus Christ for their king,
And they do not pretend
To declare their loyalty to a tyrant!

That is what they have done with fakery
In an armed encampment
Those two with a holy voice
And an animated heart;
O may their ample faith
That we hear them proclaim
Be an example to all
Who declare their love for Jesus!

May in peace and in war
All the tongues of our hearts
Sing on Earth
The praise of his greatness.
He who alone takes on himself
The burden of all sinners,
Filling them all (sweet burden!)
With the greatness of his grace.

[26r]

Dopede Poulin

Dop.

Mais un homme de bien tient tousiours sa promesse     26

P.

Si elle est contre Dieu de passer outre il cesse

D

Nous sommes resolus que de Dieu il n'est point

P

Sa crainte touteffois les meschans mord & poind

D

Ceste crainte jestime estre des sots le vice

P

Aumoins craignez le Roy armé de sa justice

D

Qui jamais luy feroit le tout au vray entendre

P

Qui? le sang des martyrs & des bruslez la cendre

D

La cendre ne le sang ne peuvent point parler

P

Le sang d'Abel a fait devant Dieu bruire l'air

D

Si les Elephans sont transformez en corneilles

*Tragedy of the Sack of Cabrières*                                           193

[26r]

Dopede, Poulin
Dop.
But a good man always keeps his promise.

P.
If it is against God to continue, he ought to cease.

D.
We firmly believe that there is no God.

P.
But the fear of God still bites and stings the evil men.

D.
This fear, I believe, is the flaw of the weak-minded.

P.
At least fear the king armed with justice!

D.
Who would ever make him hear the whole truth of it?

P.
Who? The blood of martyrs, and the ashes of the burned.

D.
Neither blood nor ashes can utter a word.

P.
The blood of Abel made air resonate before God.[1]

D.
It would be true if elephants were turned into crows.[2]

---

[1] The murder of Abel by his brother Cain, already mentioned earlier: "And He said, 'What have you done? The voice of your brother's blood cries out to Me from the ground" (Gen. 4:10).

[2] One of the many sententious remarks used by the author in this section of the text. Sententious remarks are phrases with a folkloric meaning and can stand by themselves, but are not recognized as proverbs. Many thanks to Prof. Wolfgang Mieder (German and Russian, the University of Vermont) for his help with the paroemiological aspects of the text.

P
Les rois ont longues mains grands cœurs bonnes aureilles

D
Ce qui est arresté doit tenir par raison

P
Ouy de retourner chascun à sa maison

D
Retourner on ne doit sans son dessein parfaire

P
Poursuyvre l'on ne doit en un meschant affaire          Gij

*Tragedy of the Sack of Cabrières*

P.
Kings have long hands, big hearts, good ears.

D.
What is decided must hold by reason.

P.
Yes, each must return to its own home.

D.
One shall not return without achieving one's plan.

P.
One must not pursue evil actions.

[26v]

D.

Tirez donc vostre espée & m'en donnez au cœur

P.

Ie ne seray de vous & moins d'eux le tueur

D.

Or sus D'opede sus que toymesme te tues
Quoy tu n'oses tu crains sus que tu t'esvertues
Tu tiens ta dague nue & cela est ce tout
Tu trembles ô poltron enfonces iusqu'au bout
Tu la laisses tomber or ça ie la ramasse
Et ne me puis tuer ainçois je me fais grace
Ie ne veux que la mort & si ne puis mourir
Poulin faisez le coup vueillez me secourir

P.

Il ne faut ny de soy ny d'autre estre homicide
Allons faire sonner que ce camp d'ici vuyde

D

Je vous requier un don Poulin un don petit

P

C'est quelque trahison que vostre ire bastit

D

Ce que ie demande est de nulle consequence

P

Pourveu que Dieu ou Roy nullement je n'offense

D

Aussi ne ferez vous je vous l'asseure bien

P

Dites que c'est avant que je promette rien

D

Pour sauver mon honneur d'une façon civile
Faites que m'en allant je passe par la ville
Sans y faire seiour La Composition
Telle que vous voudrez sera sans fiction

*Tragedy of the Sack of Cabrières* 197

[26v]

D.
Unsheath your sword and pierce my heart!

P.
I will not slay you, nor will I be their killer.

D.
Go, D'Opède, Go! You should kill yourself.
What, you dare not? You are scared? Then, find the courage,
You are holding your unsheathed dagger, and is that all?
You are trembling, O coward, sink it to the hilt!
You let it fall? I will pick it up for you
And then kill myself: on the contrary, I have mercy on myself!
I only want death, and if I cannot die
Poulin, please do it, please do rescue me!

P.
One should never be the killer of oneself or another.
Let us ring the bells and empty this encampment.

D.
I am just requesting a favor, Poulin, a very small favor.

P.
It is some treason, created by your anger.

D.
What I am asking for will have no consequences.

P.
As long as I offend neither God nor king.

D.
And neither you, I do assure it to you.

P.
Please say what it is, before I can promise anything.

D.
In order to save my face civilly,
Please make that, as I leave, I go through the city
Without staying there. The accord,
As you wish it, will be without falsehood

[27r]

En tout de point en point estroittement gardée
La vie si i'y faux me soit subit ostée    27

       P
Iurez vous d'y entrer seulement vous dixieme

       D
Ie renonce autrement ma foy & mon baptesme

       P
Et si tost qu'y serez d'incontinent sortir
Sans que les habitants s'en puissent ressentir

       D
Ô Terre ô mer ô puissance divine
Si aucune en y a ainsi qu'on le devine
Vous esprits familiers venez courez volez
Et en vostre courrouz auiourd'huy immolez
Sous vostre cruauté celuy qui vous invoque
Si tant peu que ce soit sa promesse il revoque

       P
Regardez que soyez constant en vos propos

       D
Pour ma fidelité vous chanterez mon loz

*Tragedy of the Sack of Cabrières* 199

[27r]

In every point, and tightly kept.
May my life be taken if I do not keep it.

P.
Do you swear to only enter the city with ten others?[1]

D.
I will renounce otherwise my faith and my baptism.[2]

P.
Do you also swear that, as soon as you are in, you will immediately leave,
Without the inhabitants noticing it?

D.
O Earth, O sea, O divine power!
If you are there, as one can presume
You, familiar spirits,[3] come, run, fly over here!
In your anger, today do immolate
In your cruelty he who is invoking you
If he ever revokes his promise!

P.
Be sure to be constant in your speech.

D.
You will sing praises to my fidelity.

---

[1] The "dixieme" here relates to a group of ten people who accompany d'Opède like an escort.

[2] Throughout his discourse, d'Opède presents himself as a man for whom religion does not matter. He does not mind swearing on faith and baptism, two of the most important elements of religion, because, from this moment, treachery and plotting to achieve his final goal matter more to him. The change is complete; the doubt-ridden d'Opède from the beginning of the play (fols. 3v–4v) is dead.

[3] Familiar spirits are, in the Bible, unholy spirits or ghosts directly under the power of Satan; they spoil whomever is in contact with them: "A man or a woman who is a medium, or who has familiar spirits, shall surely be put to death; they shall stone them with stones. Their blood shall be upon them" (Lev. 20:27).

P

Ie vais donc faire ouyr vistememement
En haut & clair sonner par le camp la retraite
Monsieur de Catderousse & quelqu'autre avec moy
Nous en allons pour vous donner a tous la foy

D

Les Capitaines sont tous de mon entreprise
Qu'en despit de Poulin la ville sera prise
Cependant que le camp feindra de s'en aller
Pour amuser mes gens leur faut encor parler

Dopede le chœur le Maire &
Le Syndique

Le Maire

Loué soit l'Eternel qui a pris à mercy
Son peuple le sauvant de ce tyran icy

Le S.        Giij

*Tragedy of the Sack of Cabrières* 201

P.
I will then have the trumpet played,
And sound high and clear the retreat from the camp.
Mr. de Catderousse and some other with me
Will go forth to deliver your oath to all.

D.
All the captains are part of my plot,
And in spite of Poulin, the city will be taken.
However, as the army will feign to leave,
In order to amuse my men, I have to talk to these people some more.

Dopede, the Chorus, the Mayor, and
the Syndic

The Mayor
Praised be the Everlasting God, who had mercy
On his people by saving them from this tyrant.

The S.

[27v]

Ô seigneur ta vertu & ta bonté est telle
Que chanter ne les peut nulle langue mortelle

### D.
Amys vous me voyez ia prest à departir
Si par les Sacremens me faites convertir

### Le M.
Dieu seul convertir l'homme & renouvelle & change
Si que d'un Diable on fait en un moment un ange

### Le S.
Pour cest œuvre il se sert ainsi que d'instruments
De sa parolle sainte & des deux sacremens

### Le M.
Dequoy la foy en nous il produit & augmente

### Le S.
La foy nostre ancre & port contre toute tourmente

### Le M.
La foy qui nous fait croire ainsi que Dieu promet
Qu'unis à son cher fils de sa maison nous met

### Le S
Nous couche en son estat et bouche à cour nous donne

### Le M.
Aux fideles Christ là sa Sainte Table ordonne

### Le S.
Christ qui a le mortel si precieux si cher
Que nostre ame il nourrit de son sang & sa chair

### Le M.
Autre nectar n'y a n'y a autre Ambroisie
Pour tousiours immortels vivre immortelle vie

*Tragedy of the Sack of Cabrières*203

[27v]

O Lord, your virtue and your kindness are such
That no mortal language can praise them enough.

D.
Friends, you see me ready to depart,
For you convert me with the sacraments.

The M.
Only God converts men, renews and changes them,
And in one moment turns a devil into an angel.

The S.
To achieve this result, he uses as tools
His holy words, as well as two sacraments

The M.
With which he produces and grows our faith.

The S.
Faith, our anchor and haven against all torments!

The M.
Faith, which makes us believe, just as God promises us,
That we shall be united with his dearest son in his home.

The S.
It hosts us in his estate and feeds us at his court.

The M.
For the faithful, Christ lays his holy table.

The S.
Christ, for whom mortals are so precious and dear
That he feeds our soul with his body and flesh.

The M.
There is no other nectar, no such ambrosia[1]
To live forever as immortals, in an immortal life.[2]

---

[1] Ambrosia, the drink of gods in Greek mythology.

[2] Sharing the blood and body of Christ is not only a commemoration of the Last
Supper, it is also the only way to have eternal life and to be saved by Christ, as seen in

Le S.

Ô viande ô breuvage en la croix appreciez
Pour donner vie aux morts tant peu soyent ils goustez

Le M.

Ainsi Dieu n'est content de nous avoir fait estre

*Tragedy of the Sack of Cabrières*

The S.
O flesh, O beverage given their value by the cross,
You give life to the dead if they taste you!

The M.
So, God is not satisfied to count us

---

John 6:51, "I am the living bread which came down from heaven. If anyone eats of this bread, he will live forever; and the bread that I shall give is My flesh, which I shall give for the life of the world," and in John 6:53–54: "Then Jesus said to them, 'Most assuredly, I say to you, unless you eat the flesh of the Son of Man and drink His blood, you have no life in you, / Whoever eats My flesh and drinks My blood has eternal life, and I will raise him up at the last day.'"

[28r]

Du ranc de ses enfans sans aussi nous repaistre 28

Le S.
Le baptesme est l'entrée en la maison de Dieu
Signe que plus bannis ne sommes en ce lieu
Comme las! paravant nous estions de nature
La sang du fils de Dieu duquel l'eau est figure
Nos ordures de l'ame efface entierement
Ordures qui causoient nostre bannissement

Le M.
Encor ce sacrement nous fait voir à l'œil comme
Nostre perversité nostre chair & vieil homme
Est mort ensevely par vertu de la mort
Et sepulchre de Christ en ce que comme mort
Le baptisé ayant l'eau jusque sur la teste
Comme enterré dessous quelque espace y arreste

Le S.
De ce qu'il en sort vif ceste nativité
Seconde le pur don de Christ resuscité
Est entendue à fin qu'à peche mort il vive
A son Dieu purement & tousiours mieux poursuyvre
Le S.Esprit en nous seul ce bien fait valoir
Nous donnant le parfaire avecques le vouloir

Le M.
Puis que ceste entrée est du tout spirituelle
La nourriture aussi n'en peut estre que telle

*Tragedy of the Sack of Cabrières*

[28r]

As his children, if he does not feed us.

The S.
Baptism is the entrance into the house of God,
As a sign that we are no longer banned there,
As, alas!, we were before by nature.[1]
The blood of the Son, of which water is a figure,
Erases entirely the filth of our soul,
That waste that had caused our banishing.

The M.
Again, this sacrament makes us clearly see
Our corruption, our flesh, and the old man[2]
Dead and buried, by the virtue of the death
And burial of Christ: in short, like a dead man,
The baptized has water all over his head,
As he is caught there, he stops there,

The S.
He emerges alive; this second
Birth, the pure reward of Christ resurrected
Is acquired, so that, dead to sinning, he may live
Purely for his God and always persevere.
The Holy Spirit in us makes this worthy,
Giving us achievement with the will.

The M.
Since this new beginning is absolutely spiritual,
Then its food itself cannot be otherwise.

---

[1] Waldensians were Baptists (the believer had to be able to profess his faith), and not pedobaptists (in which baptism is given to babies), like Catholics are. Here, we can see that since they have professed their faith, they are true believers, and then baptized, and can be truly, by their own will, welcomed in God's house. For baptism and Waldensians, see John L. Waller, "Were the Waldensians Baptists or Pedo-Baptists?" *Western Baptist Review* 4, no. 5 (1849), http://www.reformedreader.org/history/borpb.htm.

[2] A clear reference to St. Paul, and the necessity for change, to put off the old man and to put on the new. See Col. 3:9–10: "Do not lie to one another, since you have put off the old man with his deeds, / and have put on the new man who is renewed in knowledge according to the image of Him who created him."

Or la Cene est le signe apparent au dehors
Que Jesuchrist nous veut communiquer son corps
Nostre ame en substanter en l'espoir de la vie
Qui par mort ne peut estre à ses membres ravie

Le S.
Comme le pain est propre à nostre corps nourrir     Giiij
Qu'on ne peut sans manger preserver de mourir

The Last Supper is the external sign
That Jesus Christ wants to feed us his body
To sustain our soul with it, in the hope of life,
Which cannot be robbed from its members by death.

The S.
Just as the bread is proper to nourish our bodies,
And since one cannot survive without feeding,

[28v]

Le corps du Christ à l'ame est la seule viande
Qui de la mort d'enfer vivement la defende
De la mort qu'on ne peut eviter nullement
Qu'en mangeant Christ par foy spirituellement

Le M.

N[1] Son sang nostre ame aussi abbreuve & comble en joye
Tout ainsi que le vin rejiouyt nostre foye
Brief nostre ame recoit pleine refection
De son corps & son sang qui de sa passion
Nous rendent iouissans par une foy certaine
C'est où le S Esprit par la Cene nous meine.

Le S.

Nous y certifiant que Christ se donne aux siens
Si que le possedant possedant tous ses biens

Le M.

Davantage chascun fait par le saint baptesme
Profession publique & par la Cene mesme
De sa Religion par tels actes monstrant
Que Christ pour son sauveur il recognoit & prend.

Le S.

Ainsi porte l'archier le soldard le gend'arme
L'escharpe de son prince au milieu de l'alarme
Pour declarer à tous estre telle sa foy
Qu'il est prest de mourir pour l'honneur de son roy
Par les Sacremens donc tesmoigne le fidele
Qu'il est prêt de mourir pour Christ & sa querele

Le M.

Puis que d'un seul baptesme on nous a baptisez
Nous nous monstrons un corps sans estre divisez

---

[1] This capital "N" is the same as the one beginning the next stanza, which may mean that the scribe thought that this stanza was the next.

*Tragedy of the Sack of Cabrières* 211

[28v]

The body of Christ is the only meat for our soul,
Which it defends from the death of hell;
It guards from death, which can be avoided
Solely by spiritually and faithfully absorbing Christ.[1]

The M.
His blood also waters our soul, and quenches it with joy,
Just as wine pleases our liver.[2]
In short, our soul is fully satiated
By his body and his blood, which make us
Enjoy his passion with a sure faith
This is where the Holy Spirit leads us, through communion.

The S.
This certifies us that Christ gave himself to his flock,
And when we possess him, we possess all his goods.

The M.
Moreover, each one, through the holy act of baptism,
Publicly professes his religion,
And also by communion. With such actions, they show
That they accept and take Christ as savior.

The S.
That is how the archer, the soldier, and the watchman
Bear the standard of their prince in the middle of a fight,
To show all that such is their faith,
That they are ready to die for the honor of their king.
Then, through the sacraments, the faithful
Testifies that he is ready to die for Christ and his cause.

The M.
Since we were all baptized with the same baptism,
We are one whole body, with no division.

---

[1] The use of "spirituellement" can be used here as a reminder of the fact that Waldensians did not condone transubstantiation. Also, it could be an attack against Catholics, an early accusation by reformists of cannibalism (eating the body of Christ).

[2] Reference to the pleasure of drinking wine, and also of the earthly dimension of Christ's body and blood, who are first and foremost wine and bread. "Foye" here plays on the double meaning of "liver" and "faith."

Aussi un mesme pain fait de mesme farine
Mais bien de plusieurs grains ceste union designe

Just like a loaf of bread is made of the same flour,
But this union is made of various grains[1]

---

[1] A recusation of the Catholic topos that there was no unity among reformist churches. Interpretations may be different, but they all originate from the same baptism and act of faith in God.

[29r]

29

Qu'on voit en ceux qui sont unis en Jesuchrist
Comm'au chef est le corps & le corps à l'esprit

Dop.
C'est asses Je m'en vay ne vous croyant non plus
Que vous croyez au Pape aux prestres & reclus
C'est asses Je ne veux d'avantage poursuyvre
Il et temps de me joindre à mes gens pour les suivre

Le Chœur
L'on voit bien à ceste heure ô Dieu ton jugement
Lequel ton saint Prophete a crié hautement
Contre tous ceux qui ont ta doctrine haïe
Oyes Pervers oyez oyez dit Esaïe
Mais sçavez vous comment oyans n'entendez rien
Voyans & regardans ne cognoissiez le bien
Endurcissez vos cœurs pour obstinez vous rendre
Sans de vostre salue un jota comprendre
Vous oyez vous voyez & tout vous est scellé
Car le bras du Seigneur ne vous l'ha revelé

Le S.
Mais quel est ce que je voy? qu'est cela dans la fange?
Ô rencontre incroyable! helas spectacle estrange!

*Tragedy of the Sack of Cabrières* 215

[29r]

As we see among those united in Jesus Christ,
How the body belongs to the head and to the spirit.[1]

D'Op.[2]
Enough! I am leaving, since I do not believe you,
Just as you do not believe in the pope, priests, or clergymen.[3]
Enough! I do not want to continue this conversation.
It is time for me to join my people and follow them.

The Chorus
We see at this hour your judgment, O God,
Which your holy prophet cried out loud
Against all those who hated your teachings:
"Hear, you wicked ones, hear, hear!" Said Isaiah,
"Do you know how, listening, you hear nothing,
And do not know what is good while you see it and observe it?
Harden your hearts, and be obstinate,
Without understanding a thing about your salvation!
You see, you see, but everything is sealed,
For the arm of the Lord has not yet revealed it to you."[4]

The S.
But, what do I see there? What is there lying in the mire?
O unbelievable encounter! Alas, strange spectacle!

---

[1] A play on "chef," which can mean either "head" of a body, or head of a group.

[2] Many of d'Opède's lines in this part are supposed to be said aside.

[3] "Reclus" has an idea of hidden, stuck in a place, here voluntarily, with no desire to leave. I believe that here the clergymen in question must be monks or members of the regular clergy.

[4] Boccassini sees references to Isa. 29:15–22 and Isa. 42:18–19. While the whole book is based on prophetic analogies to the coming of God's reign, still not understood by weak believers, it seems to me that Isa. 48:3–5 is another reference, especially in the necessity for the people of Israel to be stern: "I have declared the former things from the beginning; they went forth from My mouth, and I caused them to hear it. Suddenly I did them, and they came to pass. / Because I knew that you were obstinate, and your neck was an iron sinew, and your brow bronze, / Even from the beginning I have declared it to you." Isa. 6:9 can also be taken into consideration: "And He said, "Go, and tell this people: 'Keep on hearing, but do not understand; Keep on seeing, but do not perceive'"

Le M.
Helas & qu'est cecy? mon Dieu le cœur me fend
C'est une femme morte embrassant son enfant
Lequel encore vif de sa petite bouche
Veut prendre le tetton de peur qu'il ne le touche
De l'un des bras la mere helas sans sentiment
Semble le reculer du mortel aliment
Aussi comme craignant que de fain il ne meure
Que signe d'un tel soin apres la mort demeure!
Semble de l'autre bras l'approcher de son sein          Hj

*Tragedy of the Sack of Cabrières*     217

The M.
Alas! What is this? My God, my heart is breaking in two!
It is a dead woman, clasping her child,
Who, still alive, with his small mouth,
Wants to suckle the nipple; for fear that he may touch it,
With one of her arms, the mother, alas!, devoid of any feeling,
Seems to push him away from this deadly nourishment,[1]
But also, for fear that he may starve
(What a sign it is that such care occurs after death!)
Seems with the other arm to bring him close to her bosom

---

[1] In "Misères," the first book of *Les Tragiques*, Agrippa d'Aubigné uses the same metaphor: "Cette femme éplorée, en sa douleur plus forte, / Succombe à la douleur, mi-vivante, mi-morte ; / ... Quand, pressant à son sein d'une amour maternelle / Celui qui a le droit et la juste querelle, / Elle veut le sauver, l'autre qui n'est pas las / Viole en poursuivant l'asile de ses bras." Agrippa d'Aubigné, *Les Tragiques*, 80.

[29v]

Pour du sang luy esteindre & sa soif et sa fain
S'il ne tette il mourra & s'il tette une morte
Voire la mort aussi par l'une ou l'autre sorte
Il ne peut eschapper Elle morte en ce point
Veut qu'il la tette, veut qu'il ne la tette point.

Le S.

J'en ay un dont ma femme est la mere & nourrice
De mere elle fera vers cestuy cy office

Le M.

Ô puissance divine à qui fais tu la guerre
Las! à qui en veux tu à un seul ver de terre
Helas! helas! voicy un trop cruel depart

Le S.

Quel ennuy vous saisit & vous tourmente à part

Le M.

C'est icy mon enfant ceste morte et ma femme

Le Chœur

Cela n'est rien voyez Cabriere est toute en flamme
Les Soldars sont entrez qui mettent tout à feu
Si subit que iamais ne l'ayons apperceu!

Le S.

Voyez la terre & l'air iusques au haut des nues
Forcener en fumé & en flambes aigues
Fut il iamais ouy ou trouvez par escrit
Si cruels ennemys que ceux de Jesuchrist

Le Chœur

Ne chante que pleurs mon Ode
Cry que le cruel Herode

*Tragedy of the Sack of Cabrières* 219

[29v]
To quench his thirst and hunger with her own blood!
If he does not suckle, he will die, and if suckles his dead mother
He will also die; either way,
He cannot escape. She, dead at this point,
Both wants him to suckle her and does not want him to suck at her breast!

The S.
I have a child, for whom my wife is both mother and wet nurse;
She will be for him a second mother.

The M.
O divine power, against whom do you wage war?
Alas! Against whom do you bear a grudge? Against a simple earthworm?
Alas, alas! This is such a cruel end.

The S.
What suffering is grasping and tormenting you so much?

The M.
That is my child; this dead woman is my wife!

The Chorus
This is nothing; see, Cabrières is entirely engulfed in flames!
The soldiers have entered, and are setting everything ablaze,
So quickly that we did not even realize!

The S.
See how the ground and the air, up in the sky,
Mangled in smoke and in blazing flames!
Has it ever been heard, or found in writing,
Of such cruel enemies as those of Jesus Christ?

The Chorus
Only sing about weeping, my ode,
Cry that the cruel Herod[1]

---

[1] Herod, king of Judea, known for the Massacre of the Innocents. When the Magi came to meet the newly born king of the Jews, Herod, fearing for his authority should a new king arise, asked them to let him know when they find him. After they meet Christ, they decide to leave, which causes the king's anger: "Then Herod, when he saw that he was deceived by the wise men, was exceedingly angry; and he sent forth and put to death all the male children who were in Bethlehem and in all its districts, from two years old or under, according to the time which he had determined from the wise men" (Matt. 2:16).

Ne fut onc si outrageux
Que d'Opede est furieux
    Le payen juif pere & mere
N'occit ne tous leurs enfans

Was never as outrageous
As d'Opède is mad.
    The pagan, Jewish father and mother
Did not kill all their children,

[30r]

N'employant sa main meurtriere
Sur ceux de plus de deux ans                                    30

Mais mon Dieu combien le passe
La cruauté de ce Thrace
Qui destruit quelle fureur!
Quelle rage quel horreur!
     Les enfans nais & à naistre
Ceux qui engendrez les ont
Et les ayeulx de leur estre
Las! par luy tous meurtris sont

Ô Roy tresheureux s'il venge
Les rapt meurtre & sac estrange
Qu'a fait ce loup furieux
Des enfans du Dieu des cieux
    Mais si tant peu soit encore
Usure il souffre ce meschant
Qui son sceptre deshonnore
Il s'en ira trebuschant

Saul perdit sa couronne
Pource que lasche il pardonne
Pensant se faire valoir
Contre Dieu & son vouloir
    Au Roy des Amalechites
Qui par sa grand cruauté
Avoit de ce monde osté
La fleur des Israelites

Mais David tout au contraire        Hij

*Tragedy of the Sack of Cabrières* 223

[30r]

And did not lay his homicidal hand
On those older than two years of age.

But, my God, he outdoes
The cruelty of this Thracian[1]
He who destroys, what furor!
What rage, what horror!
The children, born and those to come,
Those who engendered them
As well as their ancestors.
Alas, all are killed by him![2]

O happiest of kings, if he avenges
The abduction, murder, and cruel sack
Perpetrated by this furious wolf
On the children of the God in heavens!
But at least
This evil man will be worn down,
He who dishonors the scepter he serves.
He shall stumble away!

Saul lost his crown
When, cowardly, he forgave,
Thinking he would be esteemed,
Against God and his will,
The king of the Amalekites
Who, with great cruelty,
Removed from the world
The flower of Israel![3]

But David, on the contrary,

---

[1] D'Opède. Thracians were considered a warring, bellicose race.

[2] This is a fulfilling of d'Opède's promise to himself on fol. 4v to kill everyone in Cabrières.

[3] See 1 Sam. 15.

[30v]

Est l'heureux faisant defaire
Les deux qui avoient occis
Isboseth l'unique fils
    Restant de royale race
Ainsi Dieu veut que tout Roy
Des meurtriers justice face
Ou qu'il tombe en desarroy

Or le seigneur quoy qu'il tarde
Puis que sur tout il prend garde
Rendra le iuste payment
À ce meschant garnement
    Bien que des prisons il sorte
Par les juges corrompus
Les clos d'enfer ne la porte
Par luy ne seront rompus

Cependant sa conscience
Bourreau plain de deffiance
Le privant de tout seiour
Le tuera cent fois le jour
    Sans qu'il ayt nulle puissance
De mourir Au demeurant
Toute la rejioussiance
Seroit mourir en mourant

Rien n'aura qui tant luy plaise
Ne qui redouble son aise
Comme si le dard mortel

*Tragedy of the Sack of Cabrières*                                      225

[30v]

Is the fortunate one, having defeated
The two who slayed
Ishbosheth, the only son
Still in the royal lineage.[1]
Thus, God demands that every king
Lays justice on murderers,
Or that he should fall in disarray.

However, the Lord, though he delays,
Because he is aware of all things,
Will deliver just recompense
To this malicious rascal.
He may break out of prison,
Thanks to corrupt judges,
But he will not break
The gates of hell.

Nevertheless, his conscience,
A defiant executioner,
Will deprive him of any respite,
And will kill him a hundred times every day
Without him having any power
To die; in the end,
His only joy would be,
In dying, to truly die.

Nothing would please him so much
Or would double his pleasure
Than if a mortal dart

---

[1] David's faction, which has seceded, was at war against Ishbosheth's, the king of
Israel. When the latter realized that he would likely lose the war, he was assassinated by
two of his captains, who were hoping to get in David's good graces, and a reward. However, the latter could not condone regicide and had them executed. See 2 Sam. 4:9–12.

[31r]

Aux maux le livre immortel
    La mort est son espereance
Et son plus grand bien seroit
Quand pour toute delivrance
Sa mort prochaine il verroit

Les foudres & les tempestes
Parmy un troppeau de bestes
Si dru n'abattent le corps
À terre tous roides morts
    Comme le Ciel se courrouce
Et de dards pleins de venin
Vuide dessus luy sa trousse
Encor luy est trop benin

Cent pestes ja le saisissent
Mille rages l'envahissent
Mil fievres & feux ardens
Brulent jà son corps dedens
    Dejia ie le voy sans cesse
S'élancer desesperé
Et en sa plus grand destresse
Estre du sang alteré

Pour estaidre telle rage
Ne pouvant trouver breuvage
Il veut boire en un estang
Dont les sources soient de sang
    Là pour eau desalterante

31

Hiij

[31r]

Delivered him from eternal pain:
Death is his hope,
And his greatest good would be
If, for deliverance from everything,
He would see his death draw near.

Lightning and storms
Do not strike down dead on the ground
A herd of cattle,
As densely
As Heaven does in anger,
And empties his quiver
Of poisonous arrows upon him.
This would still be too kind.

A hundred plagues will hit him,
A thousand bouts of rabies will possess him,
A thousand ardent and boiling fevers
Will burn down his body inside out;
I already see him endlessly
Rush forward, desperate,
And, in his deepest distress,
Be blood-thirsty.

To smother such a rage,
Since he cannot find any beverage,
He wants to drink from a pond
Whose springs are made of blood;
There, while thirst-quenching water

[31v]

Dont il seroit soulagé
Le sang beu son feu augmente
Tant qu'il devient enragé.

J'ai de tous costez qu'il voye
Il n'appercoit que l'Orfaye
Que les morts & leurs tombeaux
Les hiboux & les Corbeaux
    Son haleine est plus puante
Que ne put un serpent mort
Ou charoigne se baignante
Au venin qui d'elle sort

Puis son sang on luy fait rendre
Pour Enfer las de l'attendre
Avec syringes & fers
Hors des veines & des nerfs
    De son corps tant deshoneste
Ains d'un mosntre si puant
Que des piez iusqu'à la teste
L'hippomaine en est fluant

Que vomiroit un tel gouffre
Mais plustost miniere à souffre
Sinon toute puanteur
Pour empunaisir le cœur
    Qui est l'homme qui devine
Tout le sang qu'il va beuvant?
Tant n'en beut d'Agrigentine
L'airain sur le feu bramant

[31v]

Would have eased his thirst,
The blood he drank amplifies the fire
So much that he is bursting with rage.

Then, wherever his gaze goes,
All he sees are vultures,
Corpses, and their tombs,
Owls and ravens;
His breath reeks more
Than a dead snake,
Or than a carrion bathing
In the venom it oozes.

And then his blood is taken,
For hell is impatiently waiting,
From his veins and nerves,
With syringes and irons
Out of his despicable body
Like a reeking monster,
From the feet to the head,
The hippomane flows out.[1]

What would such a chasm spew,
But rather a mine of sulfur,
If not all the stench
In order to infect the heart?
Who is the man who can guess
How much blood he will drink?
The tyrant from Agrigentum did not drink as much
With the bellowing bronze on fire.[2]

---

[1] The "hippomaine," generally written "hippomane," is defined in Gabriel Chappuis's translation of *Commentaire hyerogliphique ou image des choses* (Lyon: Barthélémy Honorat, 1576) by Jan Pierius Valerian, as "ce que la iument iescte dehors quand elle veut le masle" (87), which appears to be an aphrodisiac substance (what the mare ejects when she wants to attract a male).

[2] Phalaris was the tyrant of Agrigentum. A very cruel man, he was eventually overthrown and burned in his own brazen bull.

[32r]

Voy je pas dejia qu'on livre
Son ame du corps delivre                                    32
Aux enfers & aux tourmens
Et eternels grincements
    Cependant ceste famille
De martyrs victoireux
Comm'au pere plaist la feille
A Dieu plaira dans les cieux

    Poulin Le Maire Le Chœur & Le Syndique

        Poulin
Ô malheureux d'Opede! Ô Poulin malheureux!
Malheureux Catderousse! Ô soldars furieux!
Ô chrestiens bienheureux! Chrestiennes bienheureuses!
Ô combien vos morts sont devant Dieu précieuses!
Amys oyez, oyez la barbare fureur
Ô cruaute cruelle ô rigoureuse horreur!
Ie suis cause du sac: ma langue au moins confesse
Que tout ce sang par toy est espandu traistresse
Mon delict est trop grand pour en avoir pardon

        Le Syndique
Contez nous le massacre, octroyez nous ce don

        Le Maire
Ouvrez les yeux l'œil peut vous faire tout entendre
Cabriere n'est plus rien que feu fumée & cendre

        Le Chœur
Reprenez vostre aleine & nous dites comment
Vostre promesse effet n'a ny vostre serment

        Poulin
D'opede ayant cassé ce sembloit son armée
La porte ne luy est n'a dix autres fermée
        Hiiij

*Tragedy of the Sack of Cabrières*

[32r]

Do I not see, already, that one delivers
His soul, freed from his body,
To hell, to torments,
And to eternal gnashing of teeth?[1]
Nonetheless, this family
Of victorious martyrs,
Like a father is pleased by his daughter,
Will please God in the heavens.

Poulin, the Mayor, the Chorus, and the Syndic

Poulin
O unfortunate d'Opède! O miserable Poulin!
Miserable Catderousse! O furious soldiers!
O blessed Christians, men and women!
O, how your deaths are precious to God!
Friends, hear, hear, the barbarous furor,
O cruel cruelty, O severe horror!
I am the cause of the sack: my tongue, at least, does confess
That all that blood was shed because of you, O treacherous!
My offense is too great to be pardoned.

The Syndic
Recount the massacre to us, do grant us this favor.

The Mayor
Open your eyes! Your eyes can explain everything;
Cabrières is nothing but fire, smoke, and ashes!

The Chorus
Catch your breath, and please tell us how
Your promise and your oath were without effect.

Poulin
D'Opède having seemed to dismiss his army,
The gates were no longer closed to him or ten others.

---

[1] A possible reference to Luke 13:28: "There will be weeping and gnashing of teeth, when you see Abraham and Isaac and Jacob and all the prophets in the kingdom of God, and yourselves thrust out."

[32v]

Alors que l'on pensoit loin de là les soldars
Il entre & à couvert suivy par les pendars
Se saisit de la porte eux entrez à la file
Surprennent le chasteau ayant surpris la ville
Mettent le feu par tout. D'opede voit de loin
Vostre femme Syndicq' qui cachoit en un coin
Vostre petit enfant il y court tout sur l'heure
Le fait cercher à fin que l'un & l'autre meure
La mere pour son fils se presente à la mort
Prians & repriant entre ses bras le sort
Et luy dit le voyant qu'il se prenoit à rire
Si vous ne cognoissez vostre prochain martyre
Voyez que vostre mere en pleurs & larmes fond
Helas! mignon autant vous petits yeux en font
Faites bas le petit & par vostre innocence
Impuissance à parler par vostre contenance
Des larmez de vos yeux de vos tendrettes mains
Priez messieurs mignons d'estre envers vous humains
Mais quoy? la cruauté en lieu d'estre arrestée
S'enflamma de plus fort par pitié irritée
Ce que la mere obtient premiere elle mourra
Puis son enfant le tiers le pere souffrira
L'enfant pour estre yssu de diabolique secte
L'engence des serpents en l'œuf mesme est infecte.

Le Syn.
Nous sommes donc serpens puisqu'en Dieu nous croyons
Et nos petits enfans sont œufs de Scorpions

P.
On les verroit dit il qui les laisseroit croistre
"Mere il poursuyt veux tu le Pape recognoistre
"Pour celuy qui nous peut absoudre et condamner

*Tragedy of the Sack of Cabrières*

[32v]

While we thought that the soldiers were afar,
He got in, under cover, followed by his scoundrels,
And grabbed the door. They entered in a row,
Seized the castle, and, by surprise, the whole town
And set it on fire. From afar, d'Opède
Saw your wife, Syndic, who was hiding your small child
In a corner. He ran toward them immediately,
And sought them out, so that both would die.
The mother, for her son, was ready to die,
Begging and praying for his fate,
And she told him, as she noticed he was starting to laugh:
"If you do not see your approaching martyrdom,
See how your weeping mother is bursting into tears:
Alas, sweet one! As much as your small eyes can,
Shed your youth, and by your innocence,
Your inability to speak, by your face,
The tear in your eyes, your tender hands,
Pray these sweet men to be humane toward you!"
But his cruelty, instead of ceasing,
Burned even more, irritated by such pity.
What the mother obtained was that she would die first,
And then her child; the father will die last.
The child, for having been born of this devilish cult,
Is the spawn of serpents, infected in the egg.

The Syn.
So, we are serpents, because we believe in God,
And our small children are eggs of scorpions.[1]

P.
We would see, he said, who would let them grow!
"Mother," he went on, "do you wish to acknowledge that the pope
Is the one who can absolve and condemn us,

---

[1] Potential reference to Ezek. 2:6: "And you, son of man, do not be afraid of them nor be afraid of their words, though briers and thorns are with you and you dwell among scorpions; do not be afraid of their words or dismayed by their looks, though they are a rebellious house." In that case, there would be a reversal in the traditional plan, as what is evil for the Catholics (namely the "devilish cult") becomes here the staple of the true believers of God.

[32ar][1]

Et ainsi comme Dieu nous sauver & damner
Et ton fils ne sera pour ce coup mis en cendre
Mais vostre femme au lieu d'une telle offre prendre
Mon fils dit elle meure & mon mary et moy
Plustost que renoncer ô seul sauveur ta foy
Le meschant forcené de veoir un tel courage
Les fait jetter au feu pour esteindre sa rage
La mere s'escriant mon fils ô double dueil!
Ceste flamme fera de nous deux un cercueil
Petit tesmoin de Christ dans ceste flambée horrible
Vous bruslez avec moy sentant la mort terrible
Ainsi tous deux bruslans sont morts pour Jesuchrist

Le M.
Et le Seigneur au ciel a receu leur Esprit

Le Syn.
Pour le regne de Christ ô tendre creature
Mon fils tu as souffert petit la mort bien dure
Ma fidelle compaigne a monstré par effet
Que [2]Chrestienne elle estoit de parolle & de fait

Le M.
Revenez s'il vous plaist à la cruelle histoire
Par laquelle augmenter Jesuchrist veut sa gloire

P.
Apres ce j'entendi les plus grands hurlemens
J'y cours helas! c'estoyent rapts et violemens
Des filles que faisoit Pannisse dans le temple
Puis vives les brusloit. D'Opede à son exemple
Tous ceux là qu'honnoroit saintement le poil blanc
Esgorgeoit au chasteau se baignant en leur sang
Tout ce massacre il fait pour avoir leur substance
Soldars dit il soldars fait na pas qui commence
Ne pensez pas non non qu'il soit temps que cessions        Ij

---

[1] Noted as such at the manuscript website. Folio 32a has no handwritten folio number, probably meaning that the scribe forgot it during his writing.
[2] An illegible letter is inscribed there.

[32ar]

And, like God, save us and keep us from evil?
If so, then, your son will not become ashes."[1]
And your wife, instead of accepting such an offer,
Said: "My son, my husband, and I would rather die
Than renounce your faith, O sole savior!"
The evil fanatic, when he saw such bravery,
Had them thrown in the fire, to smother his rage.
The mother exclaimed: "My son, O double affliction!
These flames will be the coffin of us both!
Little witness of Christ, in this horrible inferno,
You are burning with me, feeling this excruciating death!"
Then the two of them, ablaze, died for Jesus Christ.

The M.
And the Lord in heaven welcomed their spirit.

The Syn.
For the reign of Christ, O sweet creature,
My son, you suffered, little one, such a harsh death!
My faithful companion, indeed, showed us
That she was a Christian, in words and in actions.

The M.
Please, do come back to the cruel story
Through which Jesus Christ wants to add to his glory.

P.
After this, I heard loud shrieks;
I ran toward them. Alas! There were rapes and abductions
Of young women made by Panisse[2] in the temple;
Then, he burned them alive. D'Opède, following this example,
At the castle slit the throats and bathed in the blood
Of all those who were saintly honored by white hair.
The whole massacre was organized to confiscate their belongings:
"Soldiers," he said, "soldiers, we have just begun!
Do not think, no, no! That it is time for us to stop.

---

[1] If she recognizes the authority of the pope, her son's life will be spared.
[2] See note 43.

[32av]

Tuez tuez tuez car leurs possessions
Avoir je ne pourray si quelqu'un en eschappe
Voudriez vous espargner les ennemys du Pape
Tuez souldars tuez & luy criant ainsi
Regarde ses meurtriers leur voit le cœur transy
Et de crier plus fort que cesse entre les armes
L'esgard de l'aage ou sexe ou des pleurs & des larmes
Ce vaillant Hannibal ce superbe vainqueur
Enflambant par ces cris de ses soldars le cœur
Luy-mesme les enfans avec les meres renge
Pesle-mesle enfermez[1] en une mesme grange
Craignant qu'un Orphelin eschappant de bon-heur
Ne feit un jour vuyder de son bien ce voleur
En ce lieu il enserre avec les femmes grosses
Les autres vierges (Las! quelles heureuses nopces!)
Puis il y met le feu: Or ainsi que brusloyent
La dedans ces martyrs les Meres qui vouloyent
Bien monstrer que l'amour qu'à tous apprend nature
Ne pourrait estre esteint par une mort si dure
Toutes faisans chemin par où le feu se fend
Poulsent & jectent hors chascune leur enfant
"Le trop grand amour nuyt car les meres bruslantes
En pensant les sauver des flammes violentes
Pour une seule mort deux fois les font mourir
Là ce monstre escumant encontr'eux vient courir
Et à grands coups de pique & corps & bras leur perse
Et my-rostis sanglans dans le feu les renverse
Ainsi ce petit peuple & doux & tendrelet
Ce petit peuple helas petit peuple de lait
Par glaive & feu est mort chascun sur les mammelles
Qui l'avoyent allaité un petit pouls en elles

---

[1] The middle of the word is unreadable.

# Tragedy of the Sack of Cabrières

[32av]

Kill, kill, kill! For their belongings
I will not receive, if one of them escapes.
Do you wish to spare the enemies of the pope?
Kill, soldiers, kill!" And, while he was shouting, he
Watched his murderers. His heart was benumbed,
And he shouted more loudly at them to disregard, in their killings,
Age or sex, sobbing or tears.
This valiant Hannibal,[1] this proud conqueror,
Who was enflaming the heart of his soldiers with his cries,
Lined up the children with their mothers
And haphazardly confined them in the same shed,
For fear that an orphan, lucky enough to escape,
Would one day reclaim the loot of this thief.
In this place, with pregnant women, he imprisoned
Virgins (Alas! What happy weddings!)
Then set it on fire. Then, as the martyrs
Were burning inside, the mothers who wanted
To show that maternal love, taught to all by nature,
Could not be extinguished by such harsh deaths,
Made their way to where the fire was burning,
And pushed and threw out of it each of their children.
Their too great love was harmful, because the burning mothers,
While they thought they were saving them from the violent flames,
For a single death, made them die twice.
There, this foaming monster ran toward them
And violently pierced their bodies and arms with a spear,
And, half-bloodied, half-burned, pushed them back into the blaze.
Then, these little ones, sweet and tender,
This small people, alas!, still not weaned,
By fire and weapon were killed, each still on the bosom
That had fed them; a faint pulse in them

---

[1] The Carthaginian general, who fought during the Second Punic War, was considered one of the greatest military masterminds of his time. With this comparison, one notes the final evolution of d'Opède, who went from a doubted leader in the beginning of the play, to a cunning, cruel general here.

[33r]

Dans la flambe apperceu monstroit leurs grands douleurs
Non point pour leur mort propre ains pour celle des leurs          33
Leurs bouches & leurs bras qui dedans la fournaise
Embrassoyent leurs petits en gros charbons de braise
Elles ont veu changer puis tous leurs corps en feu
Aveques leurs enfans ont plus senty que veu.

Le Ch.

Povres femmes pourquoy avez vous ésté meres?
N'ayant jamais conceu vous morts seroyent legieres
Car vous n'eussiez point veus avec vous dans le feu
Brusler cruellement vos enfans & neuveux
Ne vos enfans me vous ne feussiez morts ensemble.

P.

La mort de leurs maris à la leur ne ressemble
D'autant que ce brusleur pour rechanger d'esbat
Fait dresser dans les prez double nouveau combat
Là contr'une moytié se tenans (quelle danse)!
Ses vaillans chevaliers il fait courre la lançe
Et au sang de ceux là enferrez à la fois
Du fer jusqu'à la main chascun rougir son bois
L'autre moytié il fait (ô coeur plus dur que marbre!)
Attachez tous de ranc chascun à chascun arbre
Du haut des meurs[1] les veoit à jour ouvert perser
Et sur leurs genoux morts les testes renverser
Ils tirent contre oyez cent mille harquebousades
Contre un blanc de chrestiens ils font leurs grands bravades
Le plus pres en[2] est loin pour le moins de cent pas
Car leur mort sans languir plaisir ne donroit pas

---

[1] The "e" in "meurs" is crossed out in the manuscript, showing that the scribe realized he made a typo, and had to write "murs" (walls, ramparts) instead.

[2] The "en" is put over the two words, written in small characters.

[33r]

Glimpsed in the flame showed their great pain,
Not for their own deaths, but for that of their kin.
Their mouths and their arms, in the blaze,
Still embraced their little ones that they saw turn
Into big pieces of ember; and finally, alongside their children,
They not so much saw but felt their bodies consumed by flames.

The Ch.
Poor women! Why did you become mothers?
Had you never conceived, your deaths would be lighter,
For you would not have witnessed, in the fire,
Your children and nephews, who were cruelly put to burn with you!
Neither you nor your children would have died together.

P.
The death of their husbands is not like theirs,
Particularly as the torturer, to vary his pleasure,
Had initiated in the meadows a new battle.
There, against half the group (what a pitiful dance!)
He made his valiant knights pierce them with their lances,
And pierced from part to part, to spread their blood
Until their weapons are drenched from the blade to the hilt.
He has the other half tied up (O heart harder than marble!)
All in line, each bound to a tree.
From the top of the walls, he sees them being pierced,
And on their knees, dead!, their heads bowed down.
Hear, hear! They shot a hundred thousand bullets[1]
Against a target of Christians, with much bravado;
The closest one was at least a hundred feet[2] away from them,
Because a quick death, without suffering, would not please them!

---

[1] An "harquebousade" is the name given to the munition that is propelled from an arquebus, much like the bullets of modern pistols or rifles, which explains my word choice.

[2] Jean-François-Gaspard Palaiseau's *Métrologie universelle, ancienne et moderne: Ou rapport des poids et mesures des empires, royaumes, duchés et prinicipautés des quatre parties du monde, présenté en tableaux par ordre alphabétique de pays ou ville, et leur position géographique avec les anciens et nouveau poids et mesures du royaume de France, et l'inverse, avec la méthode pour opérer toutes les conversions par des nombres fixes, etc.* (Lyon: Lavigne Jeune, 1816) indicates that the "pied-du-roi," the official unit for a foot in ancien régime France, measured 32.66 cm (1.07 ft.).

Au reste il fait dresser la dedans un trophée
Y engrave en airain les vers d'Orphée

Iij

Besides, he installed there a trophy.[1]
On it, he engraved in bronze the words of Orpheus,[2]

---

[1] In antiquity, trophies were the corpses of defeated enemies, put in view of everyone to assert superiority. However, because of the reference to verse, I believe here the trophy in question must be a traditional representation of victory, as a cup, a vase, etc.

[2] See Ovid, *Metamorphosis*, book 10, for the legend of Orpheus and Eurydice.

[33v]

Ains les actes cruels de sa grand cruauté
Qu'il veut perpetuer à la posterité
Or Catderousse vient envoyé par Dopede
Catderousse qui tous à ce meschant vous cede
Scavez vous quelles sont ses imprecations
Ses despits maugreemens & execrations
Ô furies d'Enfer ô infernales umbres
Ô tous malins esprits foudroyans les encombres
Ô phantosmes errans avec rage & fureur
Ô vous Diables remplis d'une eternelle horreur
Ô par mes maudissons je vous consacre et voue
Ce Peuple que je quitte & du tout desavoue
Pour le bien de d'Opede & de luy & des siens
Luy renoncant le droit de tous mes anciens
Et si ce nest de cœur je vous pry qu'à cest heure
Devant tous enragé par vos tourmens je meure

Le Ch.
Du cruel insensé la priere aura lieu
Et bien tost sentira sur soy la main de Dieu
Les diables l'empliront d'une mortelle crainte
Et frayeurs de tourmens que sentira constrainte
Son ame miserable & à table mangeant
Bien tost il la rendra furieux enrageant

Le M.
Que sa mort tousiours soit aux plus grands en memoire
Pour plus ne se dresser contre le Roy de gloire

Le Ch.
Ces Chrestiens sont heureux à qui Dieu fait ce bien
Que pour son nom & loz la vie n'est plus rien
Ils ont souffert la mort pour sa sainte querele
Et il leur donne au ciel la couronne immortelle

*Tragedy of the Sack of Cabrières*

[33v]

The barbarous account of his great cruelty,
Which he wishes to commemorate for all posterity.
But Catderousse comes, sent by d'Opède,
Catderousse who yields you all to this villain.
And do you know what he invokes?
Toward what he directs his chagrin, his growlings, and execrations?
"O furies of hell! O hellish shadows
O malevolent spirits striking down obstacles,
O phantoms who wander with ire and furor,
O you devils full of eternal horror!
O, by my curses, I consecrate and dedicate
This people that I leave, and completely disavow,
For the good of d'Opède, and that of his kin,
I renounce for him the right of all my ancestors.
And, if not by heart, I beg you at this hour,
Before everyone, all in rage, by your torments I die!"

The Ch.
To this pitiful madman, a prayer will be addressed,
And soon he will feel on him the hand of God.
The devils will fill him with a mortal fear,
And with dreadful torments that, constrained,
His miserable soul will suffer; and, eating at the table,
He will breathe his last breath, furious and in rage.

The M.
May his death be forever a memory for powerful leaders
That one shall not rise up against the king of glory.

The Ch.
They are joyful, these Christians to whom God granted this gift,
That for his name and praise their life is no more!
They suffered to die for his holy cause,
And he grants them in heaven the crown of immortality!

[34r]

D'un tel diademe il a le juste Abel sacré
Aussi feut il pour luy le premier massacré
Despuis tousiours Sathan des meschans l'ire attise          34
Et contre Iesuchrist & contre son Eglise
Combien feit Jezabel de prophetes meurtrir
Et combien de martyrs Antioche flestrir
Escorcher & brusler par toute la Iudée
Pour avoir saintement la Loy de Dieu gardee
Ne voulans rien ceder à ceste vanité
Qui se mettoit devant toute divinité
Si tost que Iesuchrist est apparu sur terre
L'Ascalonite Herode à mort luy fait la guerre
Et cuidant le tuer il fait de mesme flanc
De mille enfans meurtris sortir le laict & sang
Despuis tousiours le monde a redoublé sa rage
Contre tes saints ô Christ & contre eux plus enrage
Mais tout et pour ta gloire & tel est ton vouloir
Donne nous donc pour toy de mourir le pouvoir
De Merindol le reste errant pour l'Evangile
Dans les monts & forests ne le laisse inutile
Mourir de faim Seigneur c'est ton troupeau chassé
Entre les loups receu des hommes pourchassé
Ton troupeau que dix iours la mortelle famine
Contraint de se nourrir d'escorce & de racine
Ou il en trouve il est du crud gland se paissant
Et est à ton vouloir du tout acquiesant
Ton troupeau pour te rendre iusqu'à la mort hommage
De ta vertu recoive invincible courage
Ton troupeau tant defait qu'au dedans de leurs corps
Et au travers l'on veoit le jour comme dehors
Ne veux tu regarder de ton œil amiable
Ton peuple retranché ton peuple miserable          Iiij

*Tragedy of the Sack of Cabrières* 245

[34r]

With such a diadem he crowned the just Abel;
Who was also for him the first one to be slain!
Forever has Satan aroused the ire of villains
Against Jesus Christ and his church.
How many prophets did Jezebel order to be slain?
How many martyrs withered in Antioch,[1]
Flayed and burned throughout Judea,
Because they devoutly kept the law of God,
Never willing to yield to this vanity
That put itself before all divinity?
As soon as Jesus Christ appeared on Earth,
Herod the Ascalonite[2] waged a deadly war on him
And, hoping to kill him, he drained from the same side
Blood and milk from a thousand sacrificed children.
The world has always doubled its rage
Against your saints, O Christ, and against them is ever incensed.
But everything is for your glory, since this is your will;
So grant us the power to die for you!
Do keep the people of Mérindol, wandering for your Gospel
In the mountains and forests, from dying pointlessly
From starvation, Lord! It is your hunted flock,
Welcomed by wolves, persecuted by men;
Your flock, constrained for ten days
By a deadly famine to only eat barks and roots,
When they can find some! They feed on raw acorns
And cede entirely to your will.
May your flock, to pay homage to you until the end,
Receive the invincible courage of your virtue!
Your flock, so weakened that one
Can see clear daylight through their bodies, just as it is outside,
Won't you gaze with your agreeable glance
Upon your hunted people, your miserable flock!

---

[1] These martyrs can refer to the biblical woman with her seven children (2 Mac. 7) or to historical martyrs and saints from the city or who were massacred there: Lucian of Antioch (240–312), Margaret the Virgin of Antioch (289–304), or the Martyrs of Antioch.

[2] See note 163.

[34v]

Las! ce loup acharné le mettra tout à mort
Si ta main auiourdhuy ne rompt tout son effort
Qu'encontre tous Tyrans en toy tant ils se fient
Qu'en nos cendres ton templ'un jour ils n'edifient.

Catderousse le Maire le Syndique le Chœur

Catd.

Fut il donques plaisir tel que de se venger
De ceux qui tenans bon te faisoyent enrager
Comme ce feu me plaist Neron n'en eut telle joye
Quand en Rome il voyoit derechef brusler Troye
Marchez Maire & Syndique pour accomplir mon vœu
Marchez pour estre mis tout à cest' heure au feu
Et vostre fils aussi ô captifs miserables
Faites leur compaignie innocens & coulpables
Venez y volontiers que sert le reculer
Je vous vay ensemble faire à petit feu brusler

Le M.

La constance des morts la peur en hardiesse
Nous change et fait aller mourir en grand liesse

Catd.

Le subject d'une loy autre que son Seigneur
D'estre entre les vivans ne doit avoir l'honneur

Le S.

Le fidele recoit sa mort en patience
Pour ne devoir qu'a Dieu toute sa conscience

Le M.

Mon cher fils mon enfant Dieu face en nostre mort
Que le meschant cognoisse en nos tourmens son tort

Le Ch.

Pere eternel ô Dieu avec mesm'essence
Est ton fils bien aimé ta seule sapience

*Tragedy of the Sack of Cabrières*

[34v]

Alas! This fierce wolf will put them all to death,
If your hand today does not break its effort:
Against all tyrants may they put their trust in you,
So that they rebuild your temple one day in our ashes!

Catderousse, the Mayor, the Syndic, the Chorus

Catd.
Was it such a pleasure to enact revenge
On those who infuriated you by standing firm?
How I like this fire! Nero had not such joy
When in Rome he saw Troy burn again![1]
March, Mayor and Syndic, to fulfill my promise!
March immediately into the fire,
And your son too! O miserable captives,
Be their companions: innocent and guilty,
Come with good grace, there is no use in backing down!
I am going to slowly roast you together.

The M.
The constancy of the dead turns our fear
Into boldness and makes us walk to death with great jubilation!

Catd.
The subject of a law other than his lord's
Must not have the honor to be among the living.

The S.
The faithful receives death with forbearance,
As he owes his conscience only to God.

The M.
My dear son, my child: may God in our death
Have the villain recognize his error in our torments!

The Ch.
Eternal father, O God, who has the same essence
As your beloved son, your only wisdom,

---

[1] Allusion to the Great Fire of Rome, of which Tacitus accuses Emperor Nero.

[35r]

Ton seul fils engendré de toy avant les cieux
Ton cher fils envoyé en ces terrestres lieux                    35
Pour apporter la paix aux mondains incogneue
Et nous donner la foy que les tiens ont tenue
Affranchis & sauvez par le sang de luy seul
Du regne de peché & du mortel cercueil
Du lyon rugissant de sa patte & sa gueule
Comme toy & ton fils n'est qu'une essence seule
Pere tu es en luy luy en toy est aussi
Je pri' qu'il soit en nous qu'en luy soyons aussi
A fin que sa vertu maintenant se parface
En nos infirmitez & nos pechez efface
Nous gardant à ce coup nostre cœur de faillir
Puis ce combat fini vueilles nous recueillir

Catd.
Ah c'est trop babillé marchez tant de foy dire!
Car quand le four est chauld est il pas temps de cuire

Le S.
Nous y allons Monsieur il ne faut pas tant debattre
Contre le feu chascun tout nud s'en va combattre

Catd.
Comm'ils y courent droit! Ils sont fols je le voy

Le M.
La victoire mourans nous aurons par la foy

Le Ch.
Ô souverain seigneur ô grand Dieu des alarmes
Puis que tu as si chers nos soupirs & nos larmes
Que comm'en un vaisseau tu les pens au col
Fay pour une Cabriere & pour un Merindol
Naistre & fleurir tousiours mill'Eglises en France
Qui par ta vérité deschassent l'ignorance
Des François trop seduits par l'Antechrist Romain        Iiiij

*Tragedy of the Sack of Cabrières*

[35r]

Your only son, engendered of you before the heavens,
Your dear son sent in these terrestrial lands
To bring forth the peace unknown to the worldly people,
And to give us the faith that your people have held,
Freed and saved by his only blood alone
From the reign of sin and from the deadly coffin,
From the howling lion, from his paw and his fangs,
As you and your son are by essence one.
Father, you are in him, and he in you too,
I pray that he be with us, and that we be with him too,
For his virtue now becomes reality
And erases our infirmities and sins
Preventing from that moment our heart from failing!
Then, when the fight is over, please come gather us.

Catd.
Ah, too much chatter! March, I said so many times!
For when the oven is hot, isn't it time to cook?

The S.
We are going forth, sir, there is no need to debate.
Against the fire we all go naked to fight.

Catd.
How they are running straight to it! They are insane, I can see it.

The M.
As we die, we will reach victory in our faith

The Ch.
O Lord sovereign, O great God of those who suffer,
Our sighs are so dear to you, and so are our tears,
That you wear them around your neck in the form of a vase.
May for one Cabrières and one Mérindol
A thousand churches be born and flourish in France,
Which will drive away with your truth
The ignorance of the French, seduced too much by the Roman Antichrist.

[35v]

Nous entrons en la flambe asseurez sous ta main
D'estre auiourd'huy receus en ta celeste gloire
Si tost qu'avons gousté la coupe il faut boire
Pour tousiours vivre heureux apres ce court mourir

Catd.

Entrez au feu pour veoir s'il vous peut secourir

FIN

*Tragedy of the Sack of Cabrières*

[35v]

We walk into the pyre, protected by your hand,
To be welcomed today in your celestial glory.
As soon as we have tasted the cup, we must drink it
To be happy and live eternally after this short death.

Catd.
Enter in the fire, to see if he can save you!

THE END

# Bibliography

## Manuscript of the Play

*La Tragédie du sac de Cabrières*. Vatican City, Biblioteca Apostolica Vaticana, Codex Pal. lat. 1983. http://digi.ub.uni-heidelberg.de/diglit/bav_pal_lat_1983/

## Modern Editions of the Play

Boccassini, Daniela, ed. *La Tragédie du sac de Cabrières*. In *La Tragédie à l'époque d'Henri II et de Charles IX. Première Série*, vol. 3, *1566–1567*, edited by Enea Balmas and Michel Dassonville, Théâtre français de la Renaissance 3, 203–78. Paris: Presses Universitaires de France; Florence: L. S. Olschki, 1990.

Christ, Karl, ed. *Tragédie du sac de Cabrières: Ein Kalvinistisches Drama der Reformationszeit*. Halle: Max Niemeyer, 1928.

Vianey, Joseph, ed. *La Tragédie du sac de Cabrières, tragédie inédite en vers français du XVIe siècle. Publiée avec une introduction historique par Fernand Benoit et une etude littéraire de J. Vianey*. Marseille: Institut historique de Provence, 1927.

## Other Primary Sources

Agrippa d'Aubigné, Théodore. *Les Tragiques*. Edited by Frank Lestringant. Paris: Gallimard, 2003.

Apollodorus. *Epitome*. Translated and edited by James George Frazer. Perseus Digital Library. http://data.perseus.org/citations/urn:cts:greekLit:tlg0548.tlg002.perseus-eng1:e.1.1

Aquinas, Thomas. *Summa Theologica*. New Advent. http://www.newadvent.org/summa/

Augustine. *City of God*. Edited by David Knowles. New York: Penguin Books, 1972.

Balmas, Enea, and Michel Dassonville, eds. *La Tragédie à l'époque d'Henri II et de Charles IX. Première Série.* Florence: Olschki, 1999, 5 volumes.

Boaistuau, Pierre. *Histoires prodigieuses les plus mémorables qui ayent esté observées, depuis la Nativité de Iesus Christ, iusques à nostre siècle: Extraites de plusieurs fameux autheurs, Grecz, & Latins, sacrez & profanes.* Paris, 1560.

Bodin, Jean. *Les Six livres de la république.* Edited by Gerard Mairet. Paris: Le Livre de poche, 1993.

*Bulletin du Comité des travaux historiques et scientifiques, section d'histoire et de philologie.* Vols. 3–4. Paris: Imprimerie Nationale, 1885.

Calvin, Jean. *Institution de la religion chrétienne.* Paris: C. Meyrueis, 1859.

Calvin, John. *Ioannis Calvini Opera Quae Supersunt Omnia.* Vol. 12. Edited by G. Baum et al. Brunswick: Schwetschke, 1874.

Capel, Jean. *La Doctrine de Vaudois, dressée par Claude Seyssel et Claude Coussart, avec notes dressées par Jean Capel.* Sedan, 1618.

Chaytor, H. J., ed. *Six Vaudois Poems: From the Waldensian mss. in the University Libraries of Cambridge, Dublin and Geneva.* Cambridge: Cambridge University Press, 1930.

Crespin, Jean. *Histoire des vrays témoins de la vérité de l'Évangile depuis Jean Hus jusqu'à présent.* Geneva, 1570.

———. *Histoire mémorable de la persécution et saccagement du peuple de Merindol et Cabrières et autre circon-voisins, appelez Vaudois.* Geneva, 1556.

———. *Le Livre des martyrs, qui est un receuil de plusieurs martyrs qui ont endure la mort pour le Nom de nostre Seigneur Iesus Christ, depuis Iēa Hus iusques à ceste anné presente M. D. LIIII.* Geneva, 1554.

*Documenta Catholica Omnia.* http://www.documentacatholicaomnia.eu

Erasmus, Desiderius. *The Education of a Christian Prince.* Edited by Neil M. Cheshire and Michael J. Heath. Cambridge: Cambridge University Press, 1997.

Foxe, John. *Foxe's Book of Martyrs: A Complete and Authentic Account of the Lives, Sufferings, and Triumphant Deaths of the Primitive and Protestant Martyrs in All Parts of the World, with Notes, Comments and Illustrations.* Edited by John Milner and Ingram Cobin. London: Knight and Son, 1856.

Gilles, Pierre. *Histoire ecclésiastique des Églises reformées.* Geneva: Jean de Tournes,1655.

Guettée, Wladimir. *Histoire de l'Église de France sur des documents originaux et authentiques.* Vol. 7. Paris: Redouard, 1854.

Haag, Eugène, and Émile Haag. *La France protestante ou vie des protestants français qui se sont faits un nom dans l'Histoire. Pièces justificatives.* Paris: Joël Cherbulier, 1858.

Homer. *The Odyssey.* Translated by Robert Fitzgerald. New York: Farrar, Strauss, and Giroux, 1998.

Hyginus, Gaius Julius. *Fables.* Translated by Mary Grant. Theoi Classical Texts Library. https://www.theoi.com/Text/HyginusFabulae3.html

# Bibliography

Leo X, Pope. "Decet Romanum Pontificem." Papal Encyclicals Online. Last updated February 20, 2020. http://www.papalencyclicals.net/Leo10/l10decet.htm

Marcourt, Antoine. "Articles véritables sur les horribles, grands et insupportables abus de la messe papale, inventée directement contre la sainte cène de notre Seigneur, seul Médiateur et seul Sauveur Jésus Christ." Musée virtuel du Protestantisme français. https://www.museeprotestant.org/wp-content/uploads/2014/01/Mus%C3%A9e-virtuel-du-protestantisme-Les-placards-contre-la-messe-1534.pdf

"Medieval Sourcebook: Twelfth Ecumenical Council: Lateran IV 1215." Internet History Sourcebooks Project. https://sourcebooks.fordham.edu/basis/lateran4.asp

Montaigne, Michel de. *Essais*. The Montaigne Project. https://www.lib.uchicago.edu/efts/ARTFL/projects/montaigne/

———. "Des Coches;" "Si le chef d'une place assiégée doit sortir pour parlementer." In *Œuvres complètes*, edited by A. Thibaudet and M. Rat, 876–899. Paris: Pléiade, 1962.

Montet, Édouard-Louis, ed. *La Noble leçon; texte original d'après le manuscrit de Cambridge, avec les variantes des manuscrits de Genève et de Dublin, suivi d'une traduction française et de traductions en vaudois moderne*. Paris: Fischbacher, 1888.

Peletier du Mans, Jacques. *Art Poétique*. In *Traité de poétique et de rhétorique de la Renaissance*, edited by Francis Goyet, 235–344. Paris: Librairie Générale Française, 1990.

Perugi, Maurizio, ed. *La Vie de Saint Alexis*. Geneva: Droz, 2000.

Ronsard, Pierre de. *Œuvres complètes*. Edited by Gustave Cohen. Vol. 2. Paris: Pléiade, 1950.

Sophocles. *Phyloctetes*. Translated by P. Meineck and P. Woodruff. Indianapolis: Hackett, 2007.

Virgil. *Aeneid*. Translated by John Dryden. The Internet Classics Archive. http://classics.mit.edu/Virgil/aeneid.2.ii.html

Criticism and Analysis of the Play

Baretaud, Anne. "Le Récit comme acte dans les tragédies bibliques du XVIe siècle." *Loxias* 12 (2006). http://revel.unice.fr/loxias/index.html?id=935

Klotz, Roger. "Lecture méthodique de la *Tragédie du sac de Cabrières*." *L'Information Littéraire* 46 (1994): 36–39.

Millet, Olivier. "Vérité et mensonge dans la *Tragédie du sac de Cabrières*: Une dramaturgie de la parole en action." *Australian Journal of French Studies* 21, no. 3 (1994): 259–73.

Morand Métivier, Charles-Louis. "Apprendre des massacres: Émotions et nation dans la littérature du Moyen-âge et de la Renaissance." PhD Diss., University of Pittsburgh, 2013.

———. "La Construction de la masculinité dans la *Tragédie du sac de Cabrières*: Le cas d'Opède." *Modern Languages Open* 1, no. 10 (2018): 1–14. doi:10.3828/mlo.v0i0.171.

## Studies on Theater

Biet, Christian. *Théâtre de la cruauté et récits sanglants en France (XVIe–XVIIe siècles)*. Paris: Laffont, 2006.

Bouteille-Meister, Charlotte. "Le Théâtre d'actualité d'expression française (1550–1630) ou l'impossible expression d'un dissensus?" In *Dissensus: Pratiques et représentations de la diversité des opinions (1500–1650)*, edited by Florence Alazard, Stéphan Geonget, Laurent Gerbier, and Paul-Alexis Mellet, 183–203. Paris: Champion, 2016.

Bouteille-Meister, Charlotte, and Kjerstin Aukrust, eds. *Corps sanglants, souffrants et macabres, XVIe–XVIIe siècle*. Paris: Presses Sorbonne Nouvelle, 2010.

Forsythe, Elliott. *La Tragédie française de Jodelle à Corneille (1553–1640): Le thème de la vengeance*. Paris: Honoré Champion, 1994.

Frappier, Louise. "La Topique de la fureur dans la tragédie française du XVIe siècle." *Études françaises* 36, no. 1 (2000): 29–47. doi:10.7202/036169ar

Frisch, Andrea. *Forgetting Differences: Tragedy, Historiography, and the French Wars of Religion*. Edinburgh: Edinburgh University Press, 2015.

———. "French Tragedy and the Civil War." *Modern Language Quarterly* 67, no. 3 (2006): 287–312.

Jondorf, Jillian. *French Renaissance Tragedy: The Dramatic Word*. Cambridge: Cambridge University Press, 1990.

———. *Robert Garnier and the Themes of Political Tragedy in the Sixteenth Century*. Cambridge: Cambridge University Press, 1969.

Lazard, Madeleine. *Le Théâtre en France au XVIème siècle*. Paris: Presses Universitaires de France, 1980.

Lebègue, Raymond. *La Tragédie française de la Renaissance*. Brussels: Office de la Publicité, 1983.

Leblanc, Paulette. *Les Écrits théoriques et critiques français des années 1540–1561 sur la tragédie*. Paris: Nizet, 1972.

Mazouer, Charles. *Le Théâtre français de la Renaissance*. Paris: Honoré Champion, 2002.

Reiss, Timothy. "The Origins of French Tragedy." In *A New History of French Literature*, edited by Denis Hollier, 205–9. Cambridge, MA: Harvard University Press, 1998.

Stone, Donald, Jr. *French Humanist Tragedy: A Reassessment*. Manchester: Manchester University Press, 1974.

Teulade, Anne. *Le Théâtre de l'interprétation: L'histoire immédiate en scène.* Paris: Classiques Garnier, 2021.

Teulade, Anne, and Isabelle Ligier-Degauque, eds. *La Mémoire de la blessure: Mise en fiction et interrogation du traumatisme collectif de la Renaissance au XXIᵉ siècle.* Rennes: Presses Universitaires de Rennes, 2018.

Wiles, David. *Tragedy in Athens: Performance Stage and Theatrical Meaning.* Cambridge: Cambridge University Press, 1997.

## History of the Waldensians

Arché, Jean-Guy. *Le Massacre des Vaudois du Lubéron.* Aubenas: Curandera, 1984.

Aubéry, Jacques. *Histoire de l'exécution de Cabrières et de Mérindol et d'autres lieux de Provence.* Edited by Gabriel Audisio. Paris: Éditions de Paris, 1990.

Audisio, Gabriel. "Des Pauvres de Lyon aux vaudois réformés." *Revue de l'histoire des religions* 217, no. 1 (2000): 155–66.

———. *Une Grande migration alpine en Provence (1460–1560).* Turin: Deputazione subalpina di storia patria, 1989.

———. *Migranti valdesi, Delfinato, Piemonte, Provenza (1460–1560) – Migrants vaudois, Dauphiné, Piémont, Provence.* Turin: Claudiana, 2011.

———. "Une Mutation: Les vaudois passent à la Réforme (1530–1532)." *Bulletin de la Société de l'Histoire du Protestantisme Français* 126 (1980): 153–65.

———. *Procès-verbal d'un massacre: Les Vaudois du Lubéron (avril 1545).* Aix-en-Provence: EDISUD, 1992.

———. *The Waldensian Dissent: Persecution and Survival, c. 1170–c. 1570.* Translated by Claire Davidson. Cambridge: Cambridge University Press, 1999.

Bauer, Walter. *Orthodoxy and Heresy in Earliest Christianity.* Mifflintown: Sigler, 1996.

Beneddetti, Marina, ed. *Storia del Cristianesimo.* Vol. 1, *L'età medievale (secoli VIII–XV).* Rome: Carocci, 2015.

Berthalon, Samuel, and Jean-Pierre Muret, eds. *La Doctrine des Vaudois.* Lauris: Éditions du Lubéron, 1997.

Brianson, Robert de. *L'État et le nobiliaire de Provence.* Paris: Aubin, Emeri, Clousier, 1683.

Cameron, Euan. *Waldenses: Rejections of Holy Church in Medieval Europe.* Oxford: Blackwell, 2000.

Deane, Jennifer Kolpacoff. *A History of Medieval Heresy and Inquisition.* Lanham: Rowman and Littlefield, 2011.

Godefroy, M. F. "Vers la frontière: Thomas Illyricus." In *Les Frontières religieuses en Europe du Xve au XVIIe siècle: Actes du XXXIe Colloque interna-*

*tional d'études humanists*, edited by Robert Sauzet, 89–96. Paris: Librairie Philosophique J. Vril, 2002.

Groffier, Jean. *Le Feu ardant des Vaudois*. Aix-en-Provence: EDISUD, 1981.

Gui, Bernard. *Manuel de l'inquisiteur*. Edited and translated by G. Mollat. Paris: Honoré Champion, 1926.

*Histoire de la noblesse du Comté-Venaissin, d'Avignon, et de la Principauté d'Orange, dressée sur les preuves, dédiée au Roy*. Vol. 1. Paris: David Jeune, Delormel, 1763.

Jalla, Jean. "Le Synode de Chanforan." In "Bollettino Commemorativo del Sinodo di Cianforan (Angrogna), 1532–1932," *Societa di Storia Valdese* 58 (1932): 34–48.

MacCulloch, Diarmaid. *The Reformation: A History*. New York: Penguin, 2005.

Map, Walter. *De Nugis Curialium / Courtiers' Trifles*. Edited and translated by M. R. James. Oxford: Clarendon Press, 1983.

Maynier, Balthazar de. *Histoire de la principale noblesse de Provence*. Aix-en-Provence: Joseph David, 1719.

*Mémoires de l'Académie de Nimes*. Vol. 29. Nimes: Clavel et Chastanier, 1906.

Muston, Alexis. *The Israel of the Alps: A Complete History of the Waldenses and Their Colonies, Prepared in Great Part from Unpublished Documents* [1875]. Translated by John Montgomery. London: Blackie; New York: A.M.S Press, 1978.

Parander, Jean-Jacques. *Abrégé de l'histoire des Vaudois, depuis les temps les plus reculés jusqu'à l'an 1871*. Rome: H. Loescher, 1872.

Piton-Curt, Jean-Anthoine. *Histoire de la noblesse du comté-Venaissin d'Avignon et de la Principauté d'Orange, dressée sur les preuves, dédiée au Roy*. Vol. 1. Paris: David et Delormel, 1763.

Shirley, Janet, trans. *The Inquisitor's Guide: A Medieval Manual on Heretics*. Welwyn Garden City: Ravenhall Books, 2006.

Tourn, Giorgio. *Les Vaudois: L'étonnante aventure d'un peuple-église (1170–1999)*. Turin: Claudiana, 1999.

Wadding, Luke. *Scriptores Ordinis Minores*. Rome: Novissima, 1936.

Waller, John L. "Were the Waldensians Baptists or Pedo-Baptists?" *Western Baptist Review* 4, no. 5 (1849), http://www.reformedreader.org/history/borpb.htm

Willyams, Jane Louisa. *A Short History of the Waldensian Church in the Valleys of Piedmont, from the Earliest Period to the Present Time*. London: James Nisbet and Co., 1855.

## Wars of Religion

Crouzet, Denis. *Dieu en ses royaumes: Une histoire des guerres de religion*. Paris: Champvallon, 2015.

Bibliography

El Kenz, David. *Les Bûchers du roi: La culture protestante des martyrs (1523–1572)*. Seyssel: Champ Valon, 1997.

Holt, Mack P., ed. *The French Wars of Religion, 1562–1629*. Cambridge: University of Cambridge Press, 2005.

———. *Renaissance and Reformation France, 1500–1648*. Oxford: Oxford University Press, 2002.

Jouanna, Arlette. *La France du XVIe siècle, 1483–1598*. Paris: Presses Universitaires de France, 1996.

Knecht, R. J. *Francis I*. Cambridge: Cambridge University Press, 1982.

———. *The French Religious Wars, 1562–1598*. Oxford: Osprey Publishing, 2002.

———. *The Rise and Fall of Renaissance France, 1483–1610*. Oxford: Blackwell, 2001.

Le Bas, Philippe. *Annales Historiques: France*. Paris: Firmin Didot, 1860.

Maynard, Katherine, and Jeff Kendrick, eds. *Polemic and Literature Surrounding the French Wars of Religion*. Boston: De Gruyter/MIP, 2019.

Racault, Luc. *Hatred in Print: Catholic Propaganda and Protestant Identity during the French Wars of Religion*. London, Ashgate: 2002.

Tucker, Jameson. "From Fire to Iron: Martyrs and Massacre Victims in Genevan Martyrology." In *Dying, Death, Burial and Commemoration in Reformation Europe*, edited by Elizabeth C. Tingle and Jonathan Willis, 157–74. Farnham: Ashgate, 2015.

## Studies on Renaissance Culture and Literature

Frisch, Andrea. *The Invention of the Eyewitness: Witnessing and Testimony in Early Modern France*. Chapel Hill: University of North Carolina Press, 2004.

Hassell, James W., Jr. *Middle French Proverbs, Sentences, and Proverbial Phrases*. Toronto: Pontifical Institute of Mediaeval Studies, 1982.

Jouanna, Arlette. *Le Pouvoir absolu: Naissance de l'imaginaire politique de la royauté*. Paris: Gallimard, 2013.

Jouanno, Corinne, ed. *Figures d'Alexandre à la Renaissance*. Turnhout: Brepols, 2012.

Jung, Marc-René. *Hercule dans la littérature française du XVIe siècle*. Geneva: Droz, 1966.

Knecht, R. J. *French Renaissance Monarchy: Francis I & Henry II*. New York: Longman, 1996.

LaGuardia, David P. "Two Queens, a Dog, and a Purloined Letter: On Memory as a Discursive Phenomenon in Late Renaissance France." In *Memory and Community in Sixteenth-Century France*, edited by David P. LaGuardia and Cathy Yandell, 19–36. Farnham: Ashgate, 2015.

260          *Bibliography*

Lestringant, Franck. *Lumière des martyrs: Essai sur le martyre au siècle des réformes.* Paris: Honoré Champion, 2004.

Otto, Sean A. *"Felix Culpa*: The Doctrine of Original Sin as Doctrine of Hope in Aquinas's *Summa Contra Gentiles." Heythrop Journal* 50 (2009): 781–92.

Supple, James J. *Arms vs. Letters: The Military and Literary Ideals in the "Essays" of Montaigne.* Oxford: Clarendon Press, 1984.

Thomas, Andrew L. *A House Divided: Wittelsbach Confessional Court Cultures in the Holy Roman Empire, c. 1550–1650.* Leiden: Brill, 2010.

Wolgast, Eike. *Reformierte Konfession und Politik im 16. Jahrhundert: Studien zur Geschichte der Kurpfalz im Reformationszeitalter: vorgetragen am 9. November 1996.* Heidelberg: Universitätsverlag C. Winter, 1998.

## Encyclopedias and Reference Works

Antoine-Olivier, Guillaume. *Encyclopédie Méthodique.* Paris: Panckouke, 1791.

Barjavel, C. F. H. *Dictionnaire historique, biographique et bibliographique du département de Vaucluse.* Vol. 1. Carpentras: Devillario, 1841.

Berthelin, Pierre-Charles. *Abrégé du dictionnaire universel françois et latin, vulgairement appellé dictionnaire de Trévoux.* Paris: Libraires associés, 1762.

Cotgrave, Randle. *A Dictionarie of the French and English Tongues.* http://www.pbm.com/~lindahl/cotgrave/

Monet, Philibert. *L'Invantaire des deus langues, françoise et latine.* Paris: Claude Rigaud et Philippe Borde, 1636.

Muston, Alexis. *Bibliographie historique et complémentaire de l'Israël des Alpes.* Paris: Marc Ducloux, 1851.

*The Oxford English Dictionary.* http://www.oed.com

Palaiseau, Jean-François-Gaspard. *Métrologie universelle, ancienne et moderne: Ou rapport des poids et mesures des empires, royaumes, duchés et prinicipautés des quatre parties du monde, présenté en tableaux par ordre alphabétique de pays ou ville, et leur position géographique avec les anciens et nouveau poids et mesures du royaume de France, et l'inverse, avec la méthode pour opérer toutes les conversions par des nombres fixes, etc.* Lyon: Lavigne Jeune, 1816.

Pavis, Fabrice. *Dictionnaire du théâtre.* Paris: Dunod, 1996.

Pierius Valerian, Jan. *Commentaire hyérogliphique ou image des choses.* Translated by Gabriel Chappuis. Lyon: Barthélémy Honorat, 1576.

Raçonnet, Aymar de. *Thrésor de la langue françoyse, tant ancienne que moderne.* Paris: Douceur, 1606.

Richelet, Pierre, and Pierre-Charles Berthelin. *Abrégé du dictionnaire universel françois et latin: Vulgairement appelé dictionnaire de Trévoux.* Paris: Compagnie des libraires associés, 1771.

## History of Emotions

Fivush, Robyn. "Defining and Regulating the Self through Emotion Narratives." In *Changing Emotions*, edited by D. Hermans et al., 10–16. New York: Psychology Press, 2013.

Gross, Daniel. *The Secret History of Emotions: From Aristotle's Rhetoric to Modern Brain Science*. Chicago: University of Chicago Press, 2006.

Huizinga, Johan. *The Waning of the Middle Ages*. Garden City: Doubleday Anchor, 1954.

Lewis, Michael, Jeannette M. Haviland-Jones, and Lisa Feldman Barrett, eds. *Handbook of Emotions*. New York: Guilford Press, 2008.

Marculescu, Andreea, and Charles-Louis Morand-Métivier, eds. *Affective and Emotional Economies in Medieval and Early Modern Europe*. Camden: Palgrave MacMillan, 2018.

Mathieu-Castellani, Gisèle. *La Rhétorique des passions*. Paris: Presses Universitaires de France, 2000.

Paperman, Patricia. "Les Émotions et l'espace public." *Quaderni* 18 (1992): 93–107.

Reddy, William. *The Navigation of Feeling*. Cambridge: Cambridge University Press, 2001.

Rosenwein, Barbara. *Anger's Past: The Social Uses of an Emotion in the Middle Ages*. Ithaca: Cornell University Press, 1998.

———. *Emotional Communities in the Early Middle Ages*. Ithaca: Cornell University Press, 2006.

Stearns, Peter N., and Carol Z. Stearns. "Emotionology: Clarifying the History of Emotions and Emotional Standards." *American Historical Review* 90, no. 4 (October 1985): 813–36.

## Other Sources

Berg, Henrik. "Masculinities in Early Hellenistic Athens." In *What Is Masculinity? Historical Dynamics from Antiquity to the Contemporary World*, edited by J. Arnold and S. Brady, 97–113. Basingstoke: Palgrave-MacMillan, 2013.

"Convertisseur de monnaie d'ancien régime." http://convertisseur-monnaie-ancienne.fr/

"Pope Francis Asks Waldensian Christians to Forgive the Church." *Catholic Herald*, June 22, 2015.